# The Ultimate Study Skills Handbook

# The Ultimate Study Skills Handbook

Sarah Moore,
Colin Neville,
Maura Murphy
and
Cornelia Connolly

Mc Graw Hill

Open University Press

Open University Press
McGraw-Hill Education
McGraw-Hill House
Shoppenhangers Road
Maidenhead
Berkshire
England
SL6 2QL

email: enquiries@openup.co.uk
world wide web: www.openup.co.uk

and Two Penn Plaza, New York, NY 10121-2289, USA

First published 2010
Reprinted 2011

A catalogue record of this book is available from the British Library

ISBN-13: 978-0-33-523442-4 (pb) 978-0-33-523402-8 (hb)
ISBN-10: 0-33-523442-9 (pb) 0-33-523402-X (hb)

Library of Congress Cataloging-in-Publication Data
CIP data applied for

Acquisitions Editor: Melanie Havelock/Katherine Morton
Development Editor: Jennifer Rotherham
Editorial Assistant: Della Oliver
Product Manager: Lin Gillan
Production Editor: Alison Holt

Typeset by Graphicraft Ltd
Printed in the UK by Bell and Bain Ltd, Glasgow

Fictitious names of companies, products, people, characters and/or data that may be used herein (in case studies or in examples) are not intended to represent any real individual, company, product or event.

The McGraw·Hill Companies

# Table of contents

# Detailed table of contents

# Figures and tables

## Figures

## Tables

# Guided tour

## Chapter Overview

Each chapter opens with a set of learning objectives, summarizing what knowledge, skills or understanding you should acquire from each chapter.

## Key Tips

Throughout the book you will find helpful 'Key Tips' boxes. These useful hints and tips help you succeed in your learning.

## Figures and Tables

There are a number of figures, illustrations and tables to help you visualize the concepts presented.

## Questionnaires and Activities

Awareness-enhancing questionnaires and activities have been created to help you initiate and maintain effective learning strategies.

## Exercises

Most chapters include reflective exercises designed to help you engage actively in your skills development and academic progress.

## Chapter Summary: Key Learning Points

The chapter summaries provide links to the learning objectives to help you to remember key facts, concepts and skills.

# Acknowledgements

## Authors' acknowledgements

Thanks to all at the University of Limerick's Centre for Teaching and Learning.

The authors would also like to thank Martin Sedgley, Effective Learning Service; Becka Currant and Russell Delderfield, Learner Development Unit, at the University of Bradford, for permission to use or adapt their learning resources in Chapters 3, 6, 8, 9 and 15 of this book.

## Publisher's acknowledgements

Our thanks go to the following reviewers for their comments at various stages in the text's development:

Karen Hanson, Worcester University
Andrew Matthieson, University of the West of England
Suzanne Hughes, Cardiff University
Shiela Fraser, Abertay, Dundee University
Veronica Vernon, Edge Hill
Sian Hawkins, King's College London
Christine Taylor, City University
Shirley Good, Tamworth and Litchfield College
Tim Crawford, Queen's University, Belfast
Maxine Fletcher, Oxford Brookes
Jas Sangha, Oxford Brookes

We would also like to thanks the following students for their comments:

Fiona Whitting        Penny Symonds
Thomas Walker        Jordon Jay-Taylor
Thomas Jackson       Joel Radiven
Joshua Bailey        Hannah Brown

# About the authors

**Sarah Moore** is a Professor and associate Vice President at the University of Limerick. She is author/co-author of seven books including, *The Handbook of Academic Writing* (with Rowena Murray) and *Teaching at College and University* (with Gary Walsh and Angelica Risquez). Sarah publishes regularly in peer-reviewed journals within the areas of her expertise, which include such topics as emotion and learning, teaching effectiveness, innovation in teaching and learning, academic writing and using feedback in educational settings.

**Colin Neville** is based at the University of Bradford and has worked as a lecturer, course organizer and learning development adviser in further and higher education for over 20 years. He is a visiting specialist adviser in the Learner Development Unit at Bradford and research consultant for the 'LearnHigher' referencing learning area (Centre for Excellence in Teaching and Learning (CETL) project). Colin is also the author of *How to Improve your Assignment Results* and *The Complete Guide to Referencing and Avoiding Plagiarism* (both published by Open University Press).

**Maura Murphy** is manager, programme coordinator and learner support consultant at the Centre for Teaching and Learning, University of Limerick. Among her key areas of expertise are learning preferences analysis, student coaching and essay writing. She is currently engaged in a research project that explores the essay writing experiences of new students. Maura is co-author of *How To Be a Student* (with Sarah Moore, published by Open University Press).

**Cornelia Connolly** is a lecturer in the Department of Computing and Mathematics, Dundalk Institute of Technology. Her research interests include software engineering, technology in education and numerical competency. She regularly publishes journal articles in the areas of student retention, learning dynamics, learning and pedagogical enhancement in higher education settings. Cornelia is responsible for the HEA SIF funded Individualised Digitised Educational Advisory System (IDEAs) project at Dundalk Institute of Technology.

# Introduction: How to use this book

This book will help you to develop and improve your study and learning skills at college or university. Chapters contain activities, prompts, short questionnaires and awareness-improving exercises that should help you to think more deeply about your own approaches, and to learn techniques that can help you to generate new and effective ways of learning at college. As well as reading about different themes and aspects of good study skills, this book will help you to practise a range of useful study supportive habits. This book provides:

- A set of resources, including signposts to further reading, that you can use independently as a way of supporting your active engagement with your skills development and academic progress.
- A series of interrelated chapters that will be interspersed with reflections, activities, prompts and reflective questions that will help you to initiate and maintain effective learning strategies at college or university.
- Useful new material to support your study skills, including ideas about how to communicate with experts and strategies for developing high level research, numeracy and literacy skills.

## Book overview

You can dip into and out of this text in a way that suits your priorities and needs. You do not have to read each chapter in sequence. Have a look at the overview of all the chapters below and pick the areas that are of most concern or interest to you. Over time, the challenges you face are likely to change. This book covers most of the issues that you will have to tackle, not just in the early stages of your programme of study, but through all the stages and phases of your time in higher education.

### Chapter 1: Getting into it: becoming an active, creative learner

This chapter focuses on strategies for becoming an engaged, curious, active learner. It helps you to differentiate between active and passive approaches to learning and it will help you to initiate and sustain active learning habits in your own study and learning context.

### Chapter 2: Talking to the experts: useful orientations for interacting with expert professors, tutors and lecturers

The aim of this chapter is to help you to explore and explain an issue that has rarely been given explicit attention in study skills books before now: how novices in a subject (like new students) can interact effectively with experts (like experienced tutors and lecturers). The 'novice–expert' divide can cause problems for people when they are studying, but this chapter provides you with some useful insights and techniques that can help you to bridge the knowledge gap between you and the people who teach at college.

### Chapter 3: Style matters: techniques to suit your own learning style

This chapter helps you to explore your own learning preferences, strategies and styles. Every-one is different. Learning strategies that work well for one person can be less useful for someone else. It is very helpful to be aware of ways in which you are likely to learn best and it is useful to know that there are lots of different techniques you can use to approach your studies. This chapter will help you to think about your motivation to learn, it will help you to recognize that there are different kinds of intelligence, it will help you to explore different learning techniques and to reflect on your learning effectiveness.

### Chapter 4: Taking it in and working it out: ideas for reading, listening, making notes and critically thinking about information

This chapter shows how important it is to read, to absorb and reflect on information that you will be exposed to as part of your programme of study. But information is not knowledge. While reading and remembering skills are important, they are not enough. From the very start of your studies, your approach will be much more effective if you commit to critical thinking – this means not taking information at face value. As well as good reading and information absorption skills, this chapter contains ideas about how to be a critical thinker, and it outlines a range of critical questions that are useful to ask to help you to be more analytical and searching about what you are learning.

### Chapter 5: Research skills and orientations: first steps to good research

This chapter introduces key areas of research and research methods. In particular, it explains in clear terms, those aspects of research that are often problematic for students. We help you to focus on formulating research, and deriving meaning from key observations and findings.

### Chapter 6: Getting it on paper: learning the skills for confident academic writing

Students often struggle with their writing assignments. Writing often feels like an activity that is fraught with hidden pitfalls, and it often creates huge anxieties, particularly for new students.

This chapter will help to demystify the process and to focus on how you can write with fluency, pleasure and success.

### Chapter 7: Learning the rules: punctuation, spelling, accurate referencing and avoiding plagiarism

As well as the general skills of regular, confident academic writing (which are explored in Chapter 6) this chapter gives you a comprehensive tutorial in the rules of grammar and referencing. Getting these details right can tighten your academic writing and ensure that every written assignment you submit is polished, precise and professional.

### Chapter 8: The time of your life: managing time and living life as a student

Learn ways to manage your time effectively, to avoid procrastination, to plan your studies around key events, to deal with deadlines and to generate a well-paced, anxiety-reducing approach to learning.

### Chapter 9: Learning with others: working and learning in groups

Group work can be fun and satisfying, but it can also be frustrating and difficult. This chapter will help you to maximize the advantages of group work, while minimizing the attendant frustrations and difficulties that it can sometimes cause.

### Chapter 10: Presenting in front of a crowd: learning to present your work in public

This chapter will take the terror out of pubic speaking and help you to consider effective approaches to delivering great presentations.

### Chapter 11: Keeping it together: managing stress, staying in control and being ready for exams

This chapter introduces you to some of the techniques and approaches that can help you stay physically and emotionally healthy. Studying at college or university can be stressful and difficult, and it can create new challenges that may feel pretty stressful. It will help you to consider your own approach to your health and well-being and it will show you how physical and emotional health is linked to academic performance. It also shows you that you can approach exams in ways that minimize panic and stress, and maximize your capacity to perform well and achieve the best results.

*Chapter 12: Working with numbers: mathematics and numerical competence*

Students often struggle with maths-related subjects. Maths anxiety is a known phenomenon among students at college and university. This chapter helps you to consider approaches that can support your positive orientation towards maths-related study.

*Chapter 13: Facing the future and making decisions: planning for and focusing on the rest of your life*

As well as getting through your programme of study while you are a student, you will also need to focus, ideally from the very start of your time at college, on decision making, problem solving and career planning. These are skills that you will always need, and this final chapter helps you to consider what these skills are and how best to develop them.

Throughout the book, use the range of exercises, ideas and suggestions to help you to exploit your potential and orientate you towards your studies in ways that are likely to pay off for you. We hope they will help you to recognize that even though the range of challenges you face may feel overwhelming at times, there are strategies that can help you to grapple with all these different pressures and to get the most you possibly can out of your learning in higher education.

# Getting Into It: Becoming an active, creative learner

**1**

## Chapter Contents

## Chapter Overview

- **Getting started and developing your own orientation towards active, creative learning**
- **Exploring some of the simple principles of learning that can help you to become active and engaged**
- **Considering some of the important differences between active and passive learning, creative orientations and how to get immersed**

## Introduction

You have a natural, persistent capacity to adapt to your environment. You can adapt successfully and thrive in a university setting too, but you do not have to do this in a purely pragmatic or utilitarian way. Even though there are specific tasks ahead – assignments, essays, projects, exams and other challenges – your main purpose is to learn. How well, how successful and how enjoyable that learning process is largely depends on you.

This chapter will explore some of the orientations that will help you to have satisfying and engaging learning experiences while you are at university. It will outline some of the well-documented characteristics of creative people, characteristics that we recommend you try to adopt as part of your commitment to being a student. We recommend ways in which you can inject creative and focused approaches to your work as a student.

## Some simple learning principles

There has been a lot of research about how people learn and how they learn best in higher education contexts. There are thousands of theories and principles that have emerged over the years to attempt to inform and guide tutors, lecturers and learners as to how best to orientate themselves towards their education and their learning tasks. We have extracted some of this research and below are some of the simple principles about learning that it will be useful for you to keep in mind during the course of your studies, and beyond.

First, **people are different**. You need to work to find the kind of learning strategies that work best for you. In Chapter 3 you can find out more about different learning styles and orientations to help you to identify the kinds of approaches that will help you to adopt the right learning strategies for you.

Second, **feelings matter**. Even though people are different and unique, there are some basic principles that are just part of human nature. One of these principles is that feelings make a difference to your learning. How you feel impacts on what you learn in all sorts of ways. Paying attention to your emotional and psychological health is very important. You can read more about some good strategies to help you do this in Chapters 8 and 11.

Third, **learning is a social process**. Even if you are not a wildly extraverted person, it seems almost universally true that personal relationships make a huge difference to how people behave and how they learn. Generally, when you feel part of a group, and when, as students, you feel supported by that group, you are likely to do better. It is not that learning cannot happen in unsupported hostile environments. It has and it does, but it will be much better for you if yours takes place in a context where you feel companionship, where you can interact frequently with other people, where you can hear more points of view and where other people have an interest in your learning and you in theirs.

Fourth, people work and learn more when they **feel invested** in what they are doing. In the next section Table 1.1 proposes some of the main differences between 'active' and 'passive' approaches to learning. Getting motivated, energized, engaged, enthusiastic and focused will make a really fundamental difference to your ability to learn and to the results that you achieve.

Fifth, people **do not learn best when it is all high stakes**. Learning can be defined as high stakes learning when it has immediate and potentially serious consequences for you. A lot of research shows that to learn well, you are probably going to have to encounter challenges that are difficult, uncomfortable and even stressful. But you also need space and time that is 'safe'. It is important to explore your subject and test your skills and develop your ideas in contexts where you are not worried or afraid of the consequences. Finding safe spaces to practise your skills – with peers or friends or tutors – will be hugely helpful for you to prepare for the tougher tests.

Finally, **there are no short cuts to high quality learning**. It is important to immerse yourself as much as you can, to work hard and to think deeply (see also Chapter 4). There really is no substitute for knuckling down and getting into the habit of working, studying, learning and thinking about your subjects. There will be times when the challenges feel very daunting, but committing to working hard and sticking to your schedule as much as you can will reap rewards.

| Table 1.1 Some differences between active and passive learning | |
|---|---|
| *An active approach to learning* | *A passive approach to learning* |
| Questioning – asking questions to help make things clearer, to ensure you understand, to explore aspects of a topic, to check underlying assumptions | Accepting without question – transcribing notes, not checking for understanding |
| Learning by thinking, reflecting, exploring, wondering – to enhance your own knowledge and command of a subject | Learning things off by heart, learning by rote, learning to reproduce information |
| Adopting regular habits of reading, writing, engaging with learning material | Cramming at the end of a series of lectures or before an assignment or exam |
| Integrating learning and your social life | Keeping learning and social life separate |
| Being present and engaged | Being absent and disengaged |
| Generating your own learning options and strategies | Waiting for instruction |
| Going beyond the learning materials recommended to explore aspects of the subject that particularly interest you | Sticking to the bare minimum |
| Seeking and learning from feedback | Avoiding and ignoring feedback |

### Active learning and passive learning

Table 1.1 lists some differences between active and passive learning. There are potentially vast differences between the active learning strategies in the first column of Table 1.1 and the passive learning strategies in the second. Of course there will always be times when you are rushed and distracted and have to jump hastily through some learning hoop or other during the course of your studies. But if you commit to being as active and invested in your learning as you can, the nature of your experience and the quality of your outcomes are likely to be immensely more satisfying and effective.

### Some characteristics of creative people

All education at every level should help you to find purpose and pleasure in life. Higher education should provide you with opportunities to find out more about what drives you, what you are able to do, how your skills might develop and what you are interested in. It should be focused on helping people not just to learn information and knowledge but to become creatively engaged in their lives and in their work.

Not all higher education contexts make this clear, and not all tutors or lecturers are invested in the drive to help you to be creative. But *you* always have the power to engage creatively in your learning. Csikszentmihalyi (1990) engaged in an in-depth study of a large number of creative people (artists, writers, designers, engineers and people who had clearly achieved creative breakthroughs within their domains of expertise). His analysis shows that creative people often behave in ways that contain contradictory extremes. It is worth thinking about how you might manage the following kinds of paradoxes in your own life.

### Combining physical energy with quiet and rest

Engage intensively in your work when you are in work mode, but learn to switch off completely when you are taking a break. Strike a good balance between your studies and the rest of your life. Get into the habit of working hard but also develop routines in which you can rest well and deeply.

### Not being afraid to ask 'naive' or 'stupid' questions even (or especially) when you feel you know a lot about a subject

As you develop knowledge and familiarity about your subjects, do not leave behind the skill of the novice. Sometimes simple, 'stupid' questions can be exactly what is needed to get to the bottom of a difficult issue or puzzle or question.

### Combining playfulness and discipline

It pays to be disciplined about working and studying, but discipline without playfulness or fun can very quickly become like a drudge. Creating time and space for you to play with ideas and to think in light-hearted ways about what you are learning can provide you with a novel perspective and interesting learning breakthroughs.

### Being realistic and imaginative

Creative people seem to have the capacity to adopt extremely realistic and practical approaches to their work, while also giving themselves the space and permission to let their imaginations explore the outer limits of ideas, to generate possibilities and to think beyond constraints, norms and restrictions in any field. Combining a really imaginative approach to learning along with the development of practical habits can help you to engage creatively and positively in your learning.

### Balancing extraversion with introversion

Creative people are versatile. They can withdraw from the world to reflect, retreat and think deeply about things on their own. But they also thrive on interacting creatively with the ideas and perspectives of other people. Balance the amount of time you spend talking to others, with time on your own during which you can consider your own perspectives, insights and ideas. This balance can help you to learn from others, while also generating strategies of self-containment, awareness and reflection on the other.

**Getting immersed, learning to focus, getting into 'flow'**

The more immersed and engaged you decide to become, the more likely it is that you will acquire the competencies in your programme of study quickly and effectively. Research has shown (e.g. Csikszentmihalyi 1990) that to perform as well as they possibly can, people need to feel challenged but not overwhelmed, they need to be immersed but not stressed, they need to have uninterrupted periods of time during which distractions are at a minimum and they need to feel in control.

It is more motivating to be working on something in which you feel you are stretching your skills – but it can be a fine balance. Learning challenges that feel too difficult can be demotivating – learning tasks that are too easy can just bore you and make you switch off. You need to work to find your zone – that delicate place between boredom and anxiety (Csikszentmihalyi 1990) and you need to give yourself enough uninterrupted time in that zone to allow yourself to achieve your own insights and breakthroughs.

Give yourself as many opportunities as possible to get completely immersed in what you are studying. When you create space and time for your learning, and you develop and sharpen your capacity to focus, then you will probably find lots of other surprising, exciting and positive things will happen too.

Find ways to enhance or develop your curiosity, interest and engagement from the very start of your programme of study. Ask yourself: how can I make my study and my learning as interesting as possible? Think about the things you love doing in your free time. What are your own points of reference? what are you naturally interested in? And how can you use your own experiences and knowledge to create the motivational hook that will ensure you will be happier to get immersed in a particular learning task or try to develop a dimension of expertise in your field of study. If you develop your own capacity to motivate yourself, then the quality of your learning will immediately be high, and the chances of success will be much greater. For more about developing your motivation and the drivers for your learning, look at Chapter 3.

**Developing your own active learning strategy**

Use the prompt questions below to consider the ways in which you can generate your own active learning strategy. Then check your answers against the suggestions contained in Table 1.2 near the end of this chapter.

 I can become more actively engaged in my learning in a large class setting by:

I can adopt an active learning strategy towards my course assignments by:

Active learning strategies for the subjects I already feel confident about or good at might include:

Active learning strategies for the subjects I find difficult could include:

Other ways in which I can become an active, creative learner:

Perhaps exploring these questions has triggered some ideas and strategies that you can try to adopt in different learning contexts. Not all of your studies are going to be interesting or easy. You will need to change your approach, sometimes quite radically, depending on the different subjects you are learning and the different tasks you are engaged in. But you always have the opportunity to be actively engaged: to find creative ways of thinking; to take control of your learning and to interact keenly and curiously with your programme of study.

Table 1.2 suggests some active learning orientations for various learning contexts and tasks.

| Table 1.2  Some active learning orientations in various contexts | |
| --- | --- |
| *Learning contexts/tasks* | *Active learning orientations* |
| Large class settings | Make active notes, jot down questions to follow up on later, make sure you follow up on any readings or activities recommended in class, establish or link up with a smaller group within the large class so that you can discuss the issues before or after the large class lecture |
| Course assignments | Be very clear about the criteria for marking and the nature, structure, size and shape of the assignment. Try to get access to similar assignments that have already been completed. Develop an assignment plan which clearly sets out the time required for preparation, composition and submission |
| Subjects that you are already good at | Volunteer to help others who are struggling with the subject. One of the best ways of becoming more competent in an area is to help others to learn about it |
| Subjects that you find difficult | Commit to seeking out help and assistance. Make sure that you work to gain a foothold in the subject. Be prepared to admit when you feel completely lost and develop a strategy for tackling your worries and fears. Do not avoid tackling challenges that you don't feel good at. Try to learn from your mistakes, and make sure that tutors or lecturers know that you are struggling and that you explain the nature of your struggles to them |

## Chapter summary: Key learning points

- Establish **clear goals** for yourself.
- Seek out **feedback** on your performance.
- Be clear about the **skills you already have** as well as the **skills you still need to develop**.
- Become aware of the **time** you need to allocate to different activities in your life (see detailed time management strategies in Chapter 8).
- Take good physical and psychological care of yourself so that when you are learning you can be as **relaxed and alert** as possible.
- Set up **good study habits** from the very start and **keep monitoring those habits** to make sure they are working optimally to support your learning.

### Suggested further reading

Haidet, P., Moregan, R.O., O'Malley, K., Moran, B.J. and Richards, B.F. (2004) A controlled trial of active versus passive learning strategies in a large group setting. *Advances in Health Science Education* 9(1): 15–27.

Johnson, D.W., Johnson, R.T. and Smith, R.A. (1998) *Active Learning: Cooperation in the College Classroom*. Edina, MN: Interaction Book Co.

# 2

# Talking to the Experts: Useful orientations for interacting with expert professors, tutors and lecturers

## Chapter Contents

## Chapter Overview

- **Building on your own expertise and the things you are already good at**
- **Discovering how people become experts in anything**
- **Learning how to get the most out of experts**

## Introduction

This chapter will encourage you to develop an understanding about how best you – as a relative newcomer to the subjects you are learning – can interact with your tutors and lecturers, who are likely to have developed quite advanced levels of expertise in the areas that they teach. The aim of this chapter is to encourage you to give some dedicated attention to an issue that is rarely given much practical thought in study skills literature or higher education environments: how you can talk and listen to your tutors/lecturers in ways that are more likely to bridge the novice–expert divide. It explores how you can make your tutors better at teaching you by learning to ask the right questions, by explaining and articulating your level of understanding, by using metaphors to explain how you have tried to understand a particular concept and by seeking clarification when you need it most.

We also provide you with an account of what research has discovered about the differences between novices and experts, so that you can use this knowledge to generate good approaches to developing your own expertise. We will encourage you to explore the areas in which you have expertise as well as the areas in which you feel completely new and possibly very unsure. We will also try to show that just because you are unfamiliar with a topic, does not mean that you cannot engage in very clever ways with the material and ideas that you are trying to learn about.

New students bring fantastic benefits to learning environments: they have fresh perspectives and new ideas and they adopt interesting angles on information and ideas that may have been around for a long time. Such benefits might not be exploited unless you have the confidence to ask questions, to compare new knowledge with existing knowledge, to seek out explanations and to interact in assertive ways with people who are experienced and knowledgeable.

## Reflect on things you are already good at

Think of something that you are very, very good at. Perhaps it is a physical skill or sport, perhaps it is a computer game, perhaps it is some specialized area of interest that you know a lot about. Imagine yourself engaging in that activity and reflect on the things that you do. Now imagine yourself trying to explain to someone how to do what you can do so well:

- Why are you so good at it?
- What skills have you learned about the process?
- How easy do you think it would be to show someone how to start learning the skills in which you are already an expert?

Your answers to these questions might give you some clues about why lecturers and tutors in higher education sometimes find it quite hard to teach their subjects to people who are completely new to the area. The same answers might also give you some ideas about how you can start thinking about engaging in conversations with experts in ways that support your learning.

### How you become an expert at anything

The literature on expertise and expert performance suggests that there are several things associated with the process of becoming an expert. They include the following:

- The 'ten year rule' – and what it means for your learning.
- Deliberate practice and immersion: how important they are and what they mean for your learning.
- The movement through different phases of competence.
- The development of automaticity.

Each of these features is outlined in a bit more detail below.

### The 'ten year rule' – and what it means for your learning

Did you know that to become a real expert at anything it generally takes about ten years of consistent practice? (Researchers like Simon and Chase 1973 and Ericsson 2004, along with many others, have repeatedly found this to be true across many different areas of expertise.) That might seem like a long time, but to be a real connoisseur of anything – that is what it takes.

It might be a bit discouraging to think that it takes a whole decade to master a subject area or a set of competencies and that you cannot skip the journey. Even after four solid years of study and hard work, you are still less than half way on your journey from novice to expert. Don't be discouraged by this. Moderate your ambitions about what you feel you should be able to do. Go easy on yourself. Learning is a gradual process. Of course, it takes persistence and hard work, but it also takes patience and time. Getting your degree should equip you with a range of important competencies and by the end of it you should feel high levels of competence in a range of different activities. But see yourself as someone on a learning journey that continues long after your degree has been earned.

---

**Key tip**

**It takes about a decade for someone to develop advanced expertise in a particular field or discipline**. Be persistent and work hard. But be patient too! Learning can happen in fast spurts sometimes, but the building of deep competence takes time.

---

### Deliberate practice and immersion: how important they are and what they mean for your learning

Of course it is not just the passage of time that creates experts. Learning does not happen if you sit passively at lectures and tutorials, expecting all the stuff you need to sink in through some magical process of osmosis. You do need to motivate yourself, you need to persist and engage and really work hard to learn about your subjects and to achieve your learning tasks. Learning takes time, but you need to use that time in dedicated ways: practice, testing yourself and being tested by others, becoming completely immersed in your topic is important.

Remember that you are probably going to have to work very hard, no matter what course you are enrolled on. You need to concentrate, to stay on top of your studies as much as possible, and to focus on mastering key aspects of your learning through reading, listening, writing, talking, practising and testing yourself in the subjects that you are learninng. It does not all have to be a dreadful grind though. Chapters 8 and 11 explore some of the ways you can strike a balance between work and play, and how you can stay healthy and happy in the context of all this hard work. But the evidence suggests that there is no getting away from the fact that the more of an expert you want to be, the more you are going to need to work hard as a student to gain the insights and competence that your subjects demand.

---

### Key tip

**The 'effortless genius' is generally a myth**. Even people who look like they are sailing through college are likely to be working very hard behind the scenes. And experts who make things look like a doddle may have forgotten how much work it took for them to become so proficient at the things they are good at.

---

### *The movement through different phases of competence*

The literature on expertise suggests that there are different, roughly identifiable phases on the journey to expertise and high level proficiency. These phases generally correspond to the levels of proficiency described by Dreyfus and Dreyfus (1986) as novice, advanced beginner, competent, proficent and expert or 'master' performer. The levels of proficiency framework (Dreyfus and Dreyfus 1986) has been adapted by O'Neill (2005) as follows.

*Novice*

- Rigid adherence to taught rules or plans.
- Harder to see problems 'in context' because of a lack of experience with different situations.
- Hard to make decisions using discretion.
- Limited experience base on which to integrate an assessment of challenges or problems.

*Advanced beginner*

- Can generate guidelines for action based on an awareness of some aspects of the situation.

- Situational perception is still limited.
- Some prior experience helping to build a base ready for competence.

*Competent*

- Starting to be able to cope with complexity within a field of expertise.
- More likely than beginners to see action at least partially in terms of long-term goals.
- More likely to engage in conscious deliberate planning.
- More likely to have developed a command over standardized and routine procedures.

---

### Exercise 2.1: *Which level of proficiency applies to you?*

For the subjects and topics you are learning about, which of the above profiles do you think describes you best? Where do you position yourself on this continuum from novice to expert?

| Novice | Advanced beginner | Competent | Proficient | Expert |
| --- | --- | --- | --- | --- |

 There may of course be aspects of your performance within your subjects that are closer to the expert profile than others. Reflect on what stage of expertise you are at, and try to develop a strategy that helps you move on to the next stage.

 What do these different possible stages mean for your learning at university?

You already know that it is impossible to become an expert overnight. It is also probably true that you need to move through different stages of expertise before you reach a level of high performance in any area. Remember that before something feels effortless and easy, there are probably a number of rules, routines, ideas and concepts in which you will need explicit practice.

Before you start experimenting and elaborating on your skills you need to gain control over the basic building blocks. Don't compare your performance to brilliant experts in your field. Rather try to emulate the patterns and habits of those that are just a little bit ahead of you. This is likely to give you a stronger stepping stone towards expertise.

*Proficient*

- Can see problems more 'holistically'.
- Has become more efficient at identifying most important aspects and issues associated with a problem or task.

*Expert*

- Does not rely on rules or guidelines.
- Intuitive, deep, embedded understanding of situations, an understanding that can quickly be acted on.

## *The development of automaticity*

Your tutors and lecturers are likely to exercise important skills automatically and unconsciously. When they read a journal article in their sphere of expertise, they often skim and scan very quickly and can very speedily identify the main themes, added value and conclusions of the paper. You on the other hand may need to work through scholarly material much more slowly; it may take you longer to gain an insight about what the paper is actually saying, what its key messages are, and how you might integrate that knowledge into the framework of what you already know.

This is just one example of how your approach is inevitably going to need to be different from the approach of the people who teach you. There is an additional problem associated with the 'automatic' skills that experts have acquired – and that is the difficulty associated with articulating these skills to people who are still learning them, and for which a more deliberate, slower orientation is necessary. The point is that experts may not always be the best people to ask when you are trying to understand the activities that you need to practise in order to develop your skills.

In addition, the commonly encountered finding that experts underestimate the time it will require for novices to complete certain tasks, may have important implications for you. If a tutor or lecturer says that something is simple and can be done quickly, do not be discouraged if you find that it actually feels complicated and takes longer than your tutor/lecturer suggested it might. This is a common mistake that tutors and lecturers make. Sometimes, things that eventually become easy and swift, are inevitably hard and slow when you first encounter them. Keep this in mind when interacting with experts in your higher education context.

### How to talk to experts in a way that supports your learning

Remember also that novices can still do many of the things that experts can. In the right conditions you can quickly demonstrate the foundations of competence on which experts have built more complex routines, links and ideas.

Also when you are learning from experts, remember that even those people with an enormous ocean of complicated knowledge in their heads can be understood very easily and naturally as long as the principles of natural conversation apply. So, rather than lamenting the huge gaps between your knowledge and that of your teachers, it is worth trying to create 'natural conversation' between you and them. This is not always easy to do in universities where classes are large and time is precious, but it is certainly worth looking for opportunites to have high-quality conversations with the people responsible for teaching you. Natural conversation requires an arena in which all voices have an opportunity to be listened and responded to.

### Getting feedback from tutors and lecturers

It is very important for you to get feedback from your tutors and lecturers about how you are doing. Feedback is not always easy to get, and when you do get it, it is not always heartening, but it is almost always useful and it is something you should do your best to seek out and use in whatever way you can.

Getting feedback is useful for the following reasons:

- It helps you to get a stronger sense about how you are doing on your academic programme.
- It puts your emerging skills and developing knowledge to the test.
- It helps you to get a better sense of where your strengths are and how to build on them.
- It helps you to target your energies at the areas in which you may be struggling.
- It provides you with information that can help you to reflect on how best to use your time in future.

Feedback from your tutors/lecturers is a valuable learning resource. One of the things we have noticed is that students, particularly early students, tend not to look for feedback, or, if they receive it and do not understand what it means, they are not that likely to look for clarifications or explanations. If you get a low grade on an assignment and you do not know why you got it, then that grade does not provide you with much information at all about what you can do to address particular areas of underperformance. If you get a high grade and are also mystified about why you did so well, then you may be at a loss to know how to ensure you build on the strengths that helped you to score so well.

Whenever you get a grade for an assignment – make efforts to find out the reasons for that grade. That information will help you get a stronger understanding of the criteria for performance and allow you to adapt your study time accordingly.

Negative feedback is difficult to hear, and most of us do not like listening to it. But it is a fantastic tool for analysing your performance and coaching yourself about how you can 'up your game'. So if you have done a poor assignment, remember there are very useful lessons to be learned from that, as long as you seek out and receive enough feedback to understand the reasons for the grade.

Positive feedback is also a useful and illuminating resource. If you get an A+ on any assignment, you have every reason to feeling thrilled with yourself. But also commit to analysing the reasons why you did so well, so that you can reflect on the key strengths you brought to that particular assignment and ensure you apply those strengths again. But remember also that the criteria for good performance are not the same in all subjects, and do not assume that because you have cracked it for one subject, you will necessarily have developed the skills you need to do well in other areas.

### The importance of early, formative, 'low stakes' feedback

It is very useful to get feedback about your performance *before* you have to test your skills during graded assignments or exams. If you get low stakes feedback on aspects of your learning, then it gives you time and information to allow you to improve before it has an effect on your formal grades. This is the kind of feedback that may be most difficult to get, especially if you are part of a large class. You may need to be proactive about seeking out early, low stakes feedback by asking your tutors/lecturers if they will look at a piece of practice work to see how you are doing, or by talking to other, more experienced students about your early efforts to write, solve problems, think, read and learn in your area of study. Lots of universities have learner support centres that focus on key subjects or competencies like writing, mathematics, languages and study skills. Find out where these centres are, how you can avail of them, and how they can help you to sharpen your performance.

### Initial practical tips for making contact with your teachers outside of class time

Lecturers are there to help you learn and if you need to talk to them, you should expect to be able to make an appointment or organize a meeting.

But! Keep in mind that lecturers are often very busy and many of them spend their days dashing from class to meetings to one-to-one sessions with students as well as managing their assessment, grading, research activities and administrative tasks. Check their available office hours and be prepared to recognize that they have scheduling pressures too.

Before you set up a meeting, try to figure out how much time you think you will need. Is it a small query that you think can be resolved very quickly, or is there something very difficult and involved that you need help with? It is useful to have some estimate about the 'size' of the issue you want to discuss. Some queries you have might easily be resolved by email for example, while others are likely to require more time and interaction. So remember to make use of email where possible, but also don't be timid about arranging time to meet with your teachers when you know that you are struggling.

### Recommendations and implications for your learning in higher education

You can help your teachers to learn more themselves by asking simple questions. You can help the expert to see problems in new ways and to combine ideas that have never been combined in the expert's mind before. The research suggests that as a novice student, you may be more thorough in your analysis of problems and concepts, and in this thoroughness you may find interesting possibilities and ideas that can elude the expert.

### Peer-supported learning

Recent research and practice in higher education shows that more experienced student peers can be very helpful indeed in facilitating new students' adjustment to university life and learning. Many universities have responded to this finding in order to organize peer-supported learning systems and to avail of the benefits that have been found when more experienced students interact with less experienced ones. Experienced students tend to be closer from the points of view of time, culture and perspective to novice students, yet they have also learned some of the important rules, routines and skills of academia. Co-opting experienced students as peer supports for novice students is a proven strategy and one that can help to bridge the gap between novices and experts in academic environments.

Students who have been within the higher education system for longer than you have are often ideal people to talk to if you need advice or guidance on study, learning and performance at college. On a behavioural level, talking to more experienced student peers can act as the mediator of conversations that can otherwise be incomprehensible or difficult to penetrate, and they can provide candid information to tutors and lecturers that can help teaching performance improve.

### Novice-led conversations

Many traditional academic learning environments are tutor/lecturer led. Both teachers and students can turn this around in the interests of bridging the novice–expert divide. It is useful to take the lead in learning situations: ask questions; probe lecturer perspectives; communicate with your teachers in order to demonstrate the ways in which you are navigating or not navigating the material you are expected to learn.

---

*Helping your lecturers to slow down – some useful prompt questions*

- Can you help me to understand this better by comparing it to something else?
- Can you try to rephrase what you have just said?
- Can I try to explain what I think you have said in my own words?

---

### Breaking down your academic challenges into identifiable pieces or sub-parts

Real world problems are multidisciplinary, ambiguous, poorly structured and challenging. A lot of good learning happens when you try to use your existing skills to solve a problem that you have never encountered before.

Even being required to write an essay presents a series of challenges that you will need to respond to, and it is useful to break it down into it's sub-challenges:

- An essay usually comes with a deadline – the problem of **limited time**.
- Writing the essay may require you to answer a question that you do not yet know the answer to – the problem of **researching and gaining insight**.
- Writing an essay may require you to express yourself in a particular way, according to a set of rules that you are not fully familiar with – the **problem of genre**.
- Writing an essay may require you to engage in critical thinking, to question and to explore an issue from a range of perspectives before coming to your own conclusions – the problem of **evidence-based critique**.

For each separate learning task, it is possible to identify an even more specific subset of problems and challenges that you need to get your head around. Most of these challenges involve actions that expert teachers have become very good at doing automatically. You on the other hand have the advantage of the novice, which allows you to be more aware of the different steps you will need to take to complete the task that you have been set. By breaking down each learning task, you might be able to adopt a more proactive and organized process for tackling it. Doing this can also help you to build a 'transferable skill' which will make you more competent in the face of new problems, as well as more practised in the tackling of more familiar ones.

### *Other ways in which expert–novice differences can support learning*

You are unique. There is no 'one best way' to engage in learning, and it is important for you to find the strategies that work for you. It might take you more or less time than others to read a chapter or a paper; you might be more motivated to work hard on some subjects than on others, and your own life context might determine how much time you can reasonably allocate to studying and learning.

You need to take these differences into account as you plan to interact with expert teachers in the interests of your higher education. Carroll (1963) showed that differences in time required for learning (aptitude); time willing to be spent on learning (motivation and perseverance) and time allowed for learning (opportunity) all interact to explain the differences in performance among learners.

These are the variations that require you to develop your own proactive, unique, and personal learning strategy. We know that everyone learns differently, even if they learn in the same learning contexts. As well as being aware of the differences between novices and experts, there are also substantial differences in the learning styles and strategies of individual learners (see also Chapter 3 for a detailed exploration of different learning styles and orientations).

## Chapter summary: Key learning points

- Watch experts. Study how they do things. Listen to them when they are trying to solve problems. Doing this will help you to learn to generate the best solutions yourself.
- Try to 'do something' with all of the information you encounter during your programme of study: learn actively to detect features and patterns, to link new information to frameworks you're already aware of and to adopt the critical approach we outline in Chapter 4.
- Develop your own self-monitoring skills: How am I doing? What have I learned? How can I understand this better? What information is missing? How could I solve this problem more effectively etc.
- Always be prepared to engage in dialogue with your tutors and lecturers. Be courageous about telling them the things you do not understand. Ask them to show you how they go about doing things. Tell them to slow down and explain the different steps that they might gloss over, or do automatically.

### Suggested further reading

Cho, K. (2004) When experts give worse advice than novices: The type and impact of feedback given by students and an instructor on student writing. Unpublished dissertation, University of Pittsburgh, PA.

Daley, B.J. (1999) Novice to expert: An exploration of how professionals learn. *Adult Education Quarterly* 47(4): 133–147.

Isaacs, E.A. and Clarke, H. (1987) References in conversation between experts and novices. *Journal of Experimental Psychology* 116(1): 26–37.

Moore, S., Walsh, G. and Risquez, A. (2007) *Teaching at College and University: Effective Strategies and Key Principles*. Maidenhead: Open University Press.

# Style Matters: Techniques to suit your own learning style

# 3

## Chapter Contents

## Chapter Overview

- **Discovering your intelligence type**
- **Linking your intelligence type to a range of effective learning techniques**
- **Learning how to gain the most from your study**

## Introduction

There is no one 'right' way to learn and most students develop their own strategies to help them cope with their studies. These can include techniques for managing time, reading, making notes, and writing assignments. However, it is a good idea to review these occasionally. With this in mind, this chapter introduces Howard Gardner's ideas on multiple intelligences, as your own 'intelligence type' can be connected to one or more of the learning techniques described later.

### Intelligence

Intelligence tests have been constructed traditionally around four main ability areas:

- Numerical.
- Linguistic.
- Spatial.
- Logical/reasoning.

Extending this list, Howard Gardner, a Professor of Education at Harvard University, has advanced the idea that at least eight different 'intelligences' can be identified. His ideas have significant implications for thinking and practice in the worlds of education and training (Gardner 1999, 2006). Gardner's theory will be explained in detail later, but first, please complete the eight intelligences questionnaire.

### Eight intelligences questionnaire

There are 80 questions, and you can select a response from 1 to 5 to each of them:

- **1** is the **lowest response**, usually implying a negative reaction, or no experience/no interest.
- **5** is the **highest response**, usually implying a very positive reaction/response or interest.

Work quickly through the questions and tick the response closest to your feelings on the question or statement presented.

| M | What role does music play in your life? (Listening or playing or composing) | 1 | 2 | 3 | 4 | 5 |
|---|---|---|---|---|---|---|
| K | To what extent do you enjoy sports/gym related activities? | 1 | 2 | 3 | 4 | 5 |
| L | How do you rate your interest and/or ability in mathematics? | 1 | 2 | 3 | 4 | 5 |
| S | To what extent do you enjoy building or making things out of available material? | 1 | 2 | 3 | 4 | 5 |
| W | To what extent do you enjoy games involving words, or the sounds of words? | 1 | 2 | 3 | 4 | 5 |
| P | To what extent have you had friendships that have lasted a long time? | 1 | 2 | 3 | 4 | 5 |
| I | To what extent do you have a clear sense of what you want out of life? | 1 | 2 | 3 | 4 | 5 |
| N | To what extent do you care for animals, or would like to care for them? | 1 | 2 | 3 | 4 | 5 |

| | | | | | | |
|---|---|---|---|---|---|---|
| **M** | What level of interest do you have in playing one or more musical instruments? | 1 | 2 | 3 | 4 | 5 |
| **K** | To what extent are you interested in competitive physical activity? | 1 | 2 | 3 | 4 | 5 |
| **L** | How would you rate your ability to make accurate mental arithmetical calculations? | 1 | 2 | 3 | 4 | 5 |
| **S** | To what extent do you enjoy art and/or design activities? | 1 | 2 | 3 | 4 | 5 |
| **W** | To what extent have you a personal interest in creative writing? | 1 | 2 | 3 | 4 | 5 |
| **P** | To what extent are you effective at solving human conflicts at work, home, or elsewhere? | 1 | 2 | 3 | 4 | 5 |
| **I** | To what extent are you aware of the past causes of your emotional responses to current situations? | 1 | 2 | 3 | 4 | 5 |
| **N** | To what extent have you learned about wildlife away from formal academic study? | 1 | 2 | 3 | 4 | 5 |
| **M** | To what extent do you like to sing, either alone or with others? | 1 | 2 | 3 | 4 | 5 |
| **K** | To what extent are you effective at practical tasks that require hand/eye coordination? | 1 | 2 | 3 | 4 | 5 |
| **L** | To what extent are you curious about **why** and/or **how** things work? | 1 | 2 | 3 | 4 | 5 |
| **S** | To what extent can you design and make the best use of the space around you? | 1 | 2 | 3 | 4 | 5 |
| **W** | How effective are you at bargaining or making a deal with people? | 1 | 2 | 3 | 4 | 5 |
| **P** | How well can you 'tune into' the feelings, wishes, or needs of others? | 1 | 2 | 3 | 4 | 5 |
| **I** | To what extent do you have a vision of your future career goals? | 1 | 2 | 3 | 4 | 5 |
| **N** | What role does nature and the natural world play in giving your life meaning, purpose, and pleasure? | 1 | 2 | 3 | 4 | 5 |
| **M** | To what extent does music occupy your leisure time? | 1 | 2 | 3 | 4 | 5 |
| **K** | To what extent does working with your hands give you pleasure? | 1 | 2 | 3 | 4 | 5 |

| | | | | | | |
|---|---|---|---|---|---|---|
| **L** | To what extent are you effective at designing administrative systems to manage your work? | 1 | 2 | 3 | 4 | 5 |
| **S** | How easily can you work out how to assemble something, e.g. self-assembly furniture? | 1 | 2 | 3 | 4 | 5 |
| **W** | To what extent, when others disagree with you, are you able to say what you really think or feel? | 1 | 2 | 3 | 4 | 5 |
| **P** | To what extent do you enjoy working with others in groups or teams? | 1 | 2 | 3 | 4 | 5 |
| **I** | To what extent can you predict your own response or behaviour in any given situation? | 1 | 2 | 3 | 4 | 5 |
| **N** | To what extent are you active in conserving and protecting the environment? | 1 | 2 | 3 | 4 | 5 |
| **M** | To what extent can you identify different kinds of musical instruments from their sounds? | 1 | 2 | 3 | 4 | 5 |
| **K** | To what extent do you remember best from what you have **done** (compared to seen or heard?) | 1 | 2 | 3 | 4 | 5 |
| **L** | To what extent do you enjoy mental tests or puzzles? | 1 | 2 | 3 | 4 | 5 |
| **S** | How would you rate your sense of direction? | 1 | 2 | 3 | 4 | 5 |
| **W** | To what extent do you **learn best** by discussion with others? | 1 | 2 | 3 | 4 | 5 |
| **P** | To what extent do you generally **prefer** group activity in your leisure time? | 1 | 2 | 3 | 4 | 5 |
| **I** | How would you rate your level of understanding of your weaknesses and areas for improvement in your life? | 1 | 2 | 3 | 4 | 5 |
| **N** | To what extent are you interested by natural sciences, for example biology, chemistry, physics, and geology? | 1 | 2 | 3 | 4 | 5 |
| **M** | To what extent can you remember and imitate musical rhythms and tunes? | 1 | 2 | 3 | 4 | 5 |
| **K** | To what extent do you engage in physical pursuits or exercise for pleasure? | 1 | 2 | 3 | 4 | 5 |
| **L** | To what extent do you enjoy categorizing, grouping or organizing data or information? | 1 | 2 | 3 | 4 | 5 |
| **S** | To what extent do you find that films, and other audio/visual teaching methods, are **particularly significant** ways of helping you learn? | 1 | 2 | 3 | 4 | 5 |

| | | | | | | |
|---|---|---|---|---|---|---|
| **W** | To what extent do you enjoy speaking formally in public? | 1 | 2 | 3 | 4 | 5 |
| **P** | To what extent are you an easy person to get to know? | 1 | 2 | 3 | 4 | 5 |
| **I** | To what extent do you get angry or frustrated when you fail or if things go wrong for you? | 1 | 2 | 3 | 4 | 5 |
| **N** | To what extent would you **enjoy** working in some form of environment/nature related career? | 1 | 2 | 3 | 4 | 5 |
| **M** | To what extent can you easily identify different composers just by listening to their music? | 1 | 2 | 3 | 4 | 5 |
| **K** | To what extent can you concentrate for long periods? | 1 | 2 | 3 | 4 | 5 |
| **L** | To what extent are you interested in science or solving science related problems? | 1 | 2 | 3 | 4 | 5 |
| **S** | To what extent are you accurate at judging distances between objects? | 1 | 2 | 3 | 4 | 5 |
| **W** | To what extent are you effective at explaining things logically and clearly to others? | 1 | 2 | 3 | 4 | 5 |
| **P** | To what extent would you consider yourself to be a person who easily takes advice from others? | 1 | 2 | 3 | 4 | 5 |
| **I** | To what extent do you prefer to think through your own problems, rather than seek advice from others? | 1 | 2 | 3 | 4 | 5 |
| **N** | To what extent do you **seek out** information about global environmental issues? | 1 | 2 | 3 | 4 | 5 |
| **M** | To what extent was music important to you in childhood? | 1 | 2 | 3 | 4 | 5 |
| **K** | To what extent do you prefer physical to non-physical leisure activity? | 1 | 2 | 3 | 4 | 5 |
| **L** | To what extent do you take systematic, step-by-step approaches to solving problems? | 1 | 2 | 3 | 4 | 5 |
| **S** | To what extent are you creative in a visual way, e.g. art/photography/ design? | 1 | 2 | 3 | 4 | 5 |
| **W** | To what extent are you asked to 'do the talking' by friends or fellow students in any group? | 1 | 2 | 3 | 4 | 5 |
| **P** | To what extent do you consider yourself to be a person easy for others to get to know? | 1 | 2 | 3 | 4 | 5 |

| | | | | | | |
|---|---|---|---|---|---|---|
| **I** | To what extent is **thinking** problems out alone more important than talking them out with others? | 1 | 2 | 3 | 4 | 5 |
| **N** | To what extent do you opt to relax and unwind outdoors? | 1 | 2 | 3 | 4 | 5 |
| **M** | To what extent do you discuss or listen to music in the company of others? | 1 | 2 | 3 | 4 | 5 |
| **K** | To what extent do you go out of your way to choose strenuous physical activity as a form of relaxation? | 1 | 2 | 3 | 4 | 5 |
| **L** | To what extent do you have a good memory for numbers? | 1 | 2 | 3 | 4 | 5 |
| **S** | To what extent are you observant and notice things that others miss? | 1 | 2 | 3 | 4 | 5 |
| **W** | To what extent are you good at explaining things to other people? | 1 | 2 | 3 | 4 | 5 |
| **P** | To what extent could you take the lead in discussion with a group of strangers? | 1 | 2 | 3 | 4 | 5 |
| **I** | To what extent do you look for unique or unusual ways to solve personal problems or achieve personal goals? | 1 | 2 | 3 | 4 | 5 |
| **N** | To what extent can you identify the differences between different forms of plant life? | 1 | 2 | 3 | 4 | 5 |
| **M** | To what extent do you like to discuss music with others? | 1 | 2 | 3 | 4 | 5 |
| **K** | To what extent do you enjoy any form of travel, including bus and train journeys? | 1 | 2 | 3 | 4 | 5 |
| **L** | To what extent are you effective at budgeting money? | 1 | 2 | 3 | 4 | 5 |
| **S** | To what extent can you visualize how things might look from different perspectives? | 1 | 2 | 3 | 4 | 5 |
| **W** | To what extent do you **enjoy** expressing your ideas in writing? | 1 | 2 | 3 | 4 | 5 |
| **P** | To what extent can you make people feel comfortable and at ease with you, and/or each other? | 1 | 2 | 3 | 4 | 5 |
| **I** | To what extent do you like to do things by yourself? | 1 | 2 | 3 | 4 | 5 |
| **N** | To what extent do you go out your way to read about environmental issues? | 1 | 2 | 3 | 4 | 5 |

### Scoring the questionnaire

Calculate the totals allocated to questions in each of the eight recurring code categories. The maximum score possible for any of the eight categories is 50. Write the total scores for each category in the grid and then rank your scores in the code and ranking columns.

| Questionnaire Scores | | Code | Total Score | Ranking |
|---|---|---|---|---|
| W | L | W | | |
| | | L | | |
| S | K | S | | |
| | | K | | |
| M | P | M | | |
| | | P | | |
| I | N | I | | |
| | | N | | |

The eight intelligence types suggested by Gardner (2006) are listed in Table 3.1.

| Table 3.1  Gardner's eight intelligence types | |
|---|---|
| *Code* | *Type of intelligence* |
| W | Linguistic |
| L | Logical/Mathematical |
| S | Visual/Spatial |
| K | Bodily/Physical (kinaesthetic) |
| M | Musical |
| P | Interpersonal (social) |
| I | Intrapersonal (inner) |
| N | Environment/Naturalist |

### The eight intelligences

Most of us will have some aptitude or interest in some aspects of **all** of these. But it is likely that you are more **inclined** to at least one of these eight intelligences.

| | | | |
|---|---|---|---|
| **Linguistic**  <br> This is the ability to use language in an effective way. You are likely to be particularly interested in the meanings, rhythms and influence of words in spoken and written forms. | **Logical/Mathematical**  <br> This is the ability to reason, calculate, and to think things through in a logical, systematic and analytical manner. It also involves the ability to make connections between different phenomena or activities and to understand relationships between actions. |
| **Visual/Spatial**  <br> This is the ability to think creatively in relation to space, colours, and physical forms. It includes the ability to think in three-dimensional ways and to convert these ideas into some creative form. | **Bodily/Physical (kinaesthetic)**  <br> This is about making things, or solving physically related problems. It can include also an interest in testing or competing yourself against others, for example in sport, athletics, dance, or in other ways. |
| **Musical**  <br> This is the ability to play or understand music, or be sensitive to the meanings of musical patterns and sounds, and other forms of audio communication. | **Interpersonal (social)**  <br> This is the ability to understand the motivations and actions of others. It is an intelligence that can be applied to managing others, or helping them develop their potential. |
| **Intrapersonal (inner)**  <br> This involves the capacity for honest self-analysis and reflection, including assessing your own accomplishments, reviewing own behaviour, motivations and innermost feelings. | **Environmental/Naturalist**  <br> You are likely to be actively interested and concerned with environmental issues. You are likely to be able to recognize and categorize inhabitants, features or elements of the natural world. |

(Based on Gardner 1999, 2006)

### Effective learning techniques

If you are a student on a formal course, it may seem there is little choice about **how** you learn. You may have to attend lectures and seminars at set times, in set places, and in a formal way. However, there are many opportunities to exercise your independence in the way you study, and in particular the way you do the following:

- Motivate and organize yourself.
- Manage your time.
- Work with others.
- Engage with private reading.

- Critically analyse ideas.
- Plan and write assignments.
- Revise for examinations.

As mentioned earlier, it is likely that you have already developed strategies for managing this type of independent learning. However, you are invited to look at the following range of learning techniques to see if there are any new or unfamiliar ways of learning that might appeal to you. You may find that some connect obviously with your intelligence type but others may interest you enough to try, irrespective of the result of the Gardner exercise.

## Connecting with your senses

Many of the ideas that follow draw on the basic principle of engaging your senses by using:

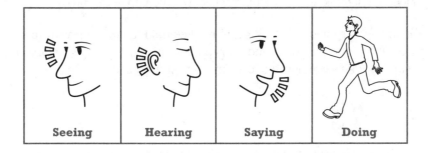

| Seeing | Hearing | Saying | Doing |

- Audio tapes.
- Free-fall thinking.
- Case studies.
- Concept maps.
- Ecology checks.
- Fishbone diagrams.
- Learning on the move.
- Making personal connections.
- Music and learning.
- Study-buddy.
- Study groups.
- Teach and learn.
- Visual notes.
- Voice notes.
- The '5W and 1H' technique.

### *Audio tapes*

Listening to audio learning tapes can be an effective way of learning for all students, but particularly for students scoring high on Linguistic and Musical Intelligence types. There is a surprising range of audio learning tapes available on the market and your library will advise what they have available, or could acquire for you.

### Free-fall thinking

Free-fall thinking a topic can be a successful approach to learning for any student, particularly when looking for solutions to case study problems or preparing for assignments. The technique may be of particular interest to students who scored high on Intrapersonal or Interpersonal Intelligences, as they will usually enjoy working with others in groups – where this approach can be very productive for generating new ideas.

You can begin by writing down a single word, phrase or full sentence. Then jot down anything you think of to capture the ideas sparked into life by the words. You could, for example, write down the problem or a question at the centre of some paper, then just write down ideas as they occur to you. Free-fall thinking is particularly effective when done in a group.

The secret is to let your mind 'run loose' and not be afraid to come up with unusual angles and responses; the motto for group and individual is 'anything goes'; workable ideas often arrive from starting with seemingly weird or impractical suggestions.

### Case studies

Using case studies can help you to explore a subject or skill in a practical way. Case studies may feature on your course anyway; but you could try converting theoretical ideas into real world case study scenarios. These can help remote and abstract subjects to come alive and give them practical meaning and application, particularly to students who scored high on Intrapersonal Intelligence.

### Concept maps

Concept maps may have a particular appeal to those who scored high on Logical/Mathematical and Visual/Spatial Intelligences. They are useful when you want to explore and build up a visual framework to answer a particular question. You start with a 'focus question', for example: 'Why do we have seasons?', and construct a network of ideas, answers or lines of inquiry; one answer can trigger off another train of thought or enquiry. The individual 'answers' or ideas are contained within boxes, linked by a network of connecting words or phrases, e.g. **Seasons** . . . *are determined by* . . . **Amount of Sunlight** . . . *is determined by* . . . and so on. See the example in Figure 3.1 (Novak and Canãs 2006).

The advantage of building concept maps is that they can:

- help you to identify what you know on a topic, and what you need to learn.
- provide a visual framework for connecting ideas.
- help you to remember the whole picture more easily.

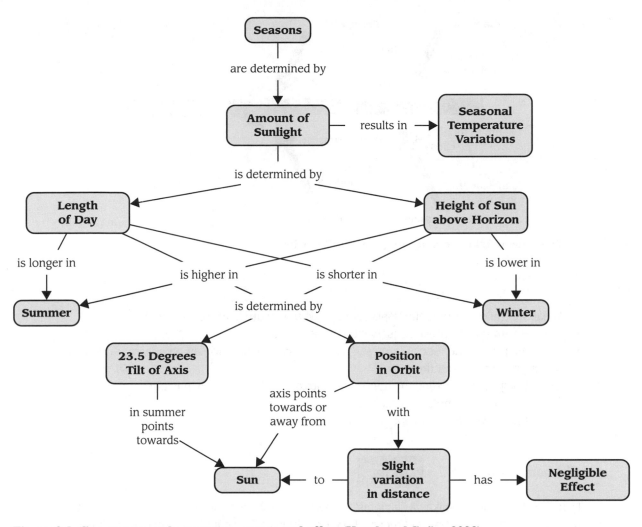

**Figure 3.1  Concept map: the seasons – cause and effect (Novak and Cañas 2006)**

You can find out more about concept mapping and download free software from the website of IHMC Cmap Tools at **http://cmap.ihmc.us/conceptmap.html**

See also **'Fishbone diagrams'** and **'Visual notes'** in this chapter.

### *Ecology checks*

Ecology checks may appeal particularly to students who scored high on Environmental Intelligence type. If you did, it is likely that you will be concerned about the impact or effect of any particular subject on the world and people who live in it. If that is so, Rose and Nicholl (1997) suggest you to run an 'ecological' check on any relevant topic, and ask the following questions:

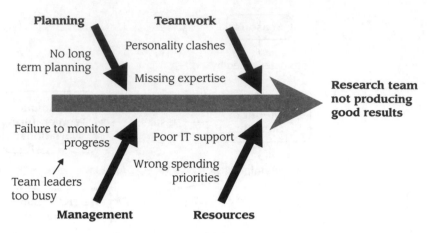

**Figure 3.2 Example of fishbone diagram (Lau and Chan 2006)**

- What are the environmental implications of what you are learning?
- Has it any implications for conservation of resources?
- Will it help or hinder social fairness? Does it have anything to say on solving any of the major problems of our times?
- Does it help to understand the mind of individuals or their social behaviour?
- Does it exploit anyone or anything else?
- Does it guide you to any action or social purpose?

### Fishbone diagrams

Fishbone diagrams or 'Ishikawa diagrams' (named after Professor Kaoru Ishikawa, the originator) may have a particular appeal to those who scored high on Logical/Mathematical and Visual/Spatial Intelligences. They are useful for analysis to identify and illustrate cause and effect issues in any problematic situation. The problem is identified (tip of arrow) and 'side bones' are added, as appropriate, to build up a structure of possible causes contributing to the 'effect' (see Figure 3.2). Fishbone diagrams are useful both as a focus for group discussion and as an individual form of visual note making. See also **'Concept maps'** and **'Visual notes'** in this chapter.

### Learning on the move

The technique of learning on the move may appeal to those who scored high on Bodily/Physical Intelligence. If you dislike sitting still for too long to study, take advantage of a journey (bus, train etc.) to read books or your notes. If you study while you travel, you can read for a while, observe the passing scene when you get bored, then return to your reading.

### *Making personal connections*

Making personal connections is about creating a personal interest in any subject you perceive as boring. This can be a particular issue for those who scored high on Intrapersonal Intelligence. They will usually give 100 per cent of their attention to subjects which interest them, but the converse can apply if the subjects are perceived as irrelevant to their lives. The way forward, if you are in this situation, is to try to find a **connection** between the subject and your own life, and to explore the subject at a **personal** level. This may seem difficult, but it can be done, in the following ways:

- You will learn better and make any subject more interesting if you ask yourself: How can I use this idea? What personal significance can I find in this for me?
- Reflect on **why** you find some subjects or learning situations difficult. You will probably find this connects with past negative experiences. If you have unpleasant memories from the past of a particular subject, you may still feel negatively about it today. But you can change the way you perceive the situation – you do not **have** to feel bad about it now. The past is the past, now is now.
- Think about the reasons behind the development of the idea, theory or practice: Why did it appear on the scene? What is the history behind it?
- If you had to summarize the main points of a particular theory, idea or practice for a group of people who knew nothing of the subject, what would you say? How would you do it?
- Ask lecturers why they find these subjects so interesting and encourage them to share some of their interest with you. Many lecturers are quietly passionate about their subject area and are often very happy to explain why. The discussion you have, and the sharing of ideas in this way, may ignite a spark of interest for you.

### *Music and learning*

Music plays an important role in learning, and not just for those who scored highly on Musical Intelligence. Remember the songs you learned at primary school. These were not just for entertainment, but were included in the curriculum to develop your language, memory, arithmetic, colour recognition and common societal values. In adult life music can play a role in enhancing learning, although exactly how it does this is still a matter for research. For example, it has been asserted that listening to Baroque classical music can create the right conditions to help some people learn. It may be that the associations of reading, linked to a relaxed state induced by the music, may help some students to recall the main points of a topic (Dickinson 1997). Why not test this for yourself?

There is some evidence, too, that **participation** in music making can aid memory; for example, musically trained adults appear to perform better on verbal word memory tests than other adults (Franklin et al. 2008). What role does music play in your life? Can you connect an interest in music to effective learning techniques? For example, could you link a list of items to a mnemonic, assisted by a particular rhythm or rhyme? Or could you memorize a particular theory by building a song melody around the ideas? In factories during the Second World War and afterwards, music was often played to lift morale – and speed production. Could music speed your creative thinking? Could music that gradually builds the tempo, such as Ravel's *Bolero*, connect with the way creative ideas emerge individually or in a group? Try it and see.

### Study-buddy

Find another student on the same course (a 'study-buddy') and meet regularly to talk through the main points from a lecture, seminar or set reading. You can, for example, share out reading with your study-buddy. You and your buddy agree to read a chapter each then meet to tell each other about it.

### Study groups

Study groups can work for all students, but particularly those who scored highly on Inter-personal Intelligence, as they work on the same principle as the study-buddy idea. Your group will meet on a regular basis and with a pre-agreed agenda. You could, for example, agree to review a particular lecture, read a selected chapter of a set book, or discuss an essay topic.

### Teach and learn

One of the best ways for students to learn, particularly those with high scores in Interpersonal Intelligence, is to teach – or at least explain to – others what they have learned. When you have to explain things to others, you start to think hard and seriously about it. Talking to other people about a subject requires you to organize your thoughts into a logical sequence. You also have to take into account the other people's ability, grasp of language, and knowledge, which makes you refine the way you present the subject to them. This can reinforce your own knowledge.

The **study-buddy** or **study group** ideas suggested earlier give you an opportunity to do this, but your institution may run a **mentoring** or **peer assisted learning (PAL)** programme, which could give you the chance formally to help new students (or 'mentees') with their studies. Mentors offer four key support roles to mentees:

- Inducting new students into 'the system' and thereby helping them gain confidence more quickly.
- Passing knowledge on to mentees: for example, as to what tutors are looking for in assignments and other assessed work.
- Helping mentees develop techniques for effective learning.
- Giving practical and useful information to mentees on coping independently away from home.

## *Visual notes*

One effective learning technique that can appeal to students who score highly on Visual/Spatial Intelligence is make notes more visual (see Figure 3.3). This form of note taking allows you to visually connect ideas to overview a topic. You can add your own observations and critical comments to the notes.

Some ideas seem very feasible, as you can see the trend already, e.g. home working; However, brain implants ... not sure, but technology is rapidly advancing, so it could be possible in 50 years' time – but who would want a brain implant, even then!

Individual choices will become more important; role of Internet more prominent in serving individual lifestyle choices; role of women will become more significant in the workplace.

We will gain more control over our bodies; particularly our brains; gain more access to legalized drugs to improve memory/enhance pleasure; longevity will increase to 100+.

**A short history of the future** report based on predictions by 5000+ organizations on what world would look like in 2050.

Service sector work will expand; movement away from work in large companies; employers will need to make jobs more attractive to retain key staff.

Microchip implants in our brains will develop our abilities to communicate with others and we will be able to store aspects of our selves, e.g. memories, in databanks.

Communication systems will encourage more electronic communications, e.g. 3-D systems, between people on an everyday basis.

This will escalate the trend to home working, which in turn will encourage development of community life; may reduce numbers of houses for sale or rent (less mobility).

Figure 3.3 **Example of visual notes**

### Voice notes

The voice notes technique may particularly appeal to those with high Linguistic Intelligence scores.

- Using a voice-recorder to summarize ideas verbally can work well for some students, as it can help them to concentrate on reading.
- The process of verbally summarizing what you have read, heard or seen can help you to focus on the main points and select the right words to express a particular idea.
- The tapes made can be replayed in situations away from formal learning areas; for example, you can listen while you exercise, drive or travel on public transport.

### The '5W and 1H' technique

The 5W and 1H technique refers to six questions: Who? What? Where? Why? When? How?

This type of technique can have a particular appeal to anyone scoring high on Logical/ Mathematical Intelligence, although the questioning process is at the heart of critical analysis, which makes it a useful approach for **all** students. You apply the technique by asking interrogative questions of any idea, model, or practice in preparation for tutorials or writing assignments (see Table 3.2).

| Table 3.2 The 5W and 1H technique | |
|---|---|
| **Who?** | **Who** is the idea aimed at? Who might benefit or be disadvantaged by the idea? Who is or is not involved? Who developed the idea? |
| **What?** | **What** are we taking for granted? What assumptions, if any, are we making? What is implied that may not be true? What is missing? What is the background to this idea? What is the wider significance of the idea? What are the advantages and negatives of the idea? |
| **Where?** | **Where** did the idea originate? Where can it be applied? Where would it not be applicable? (Are there, for example, cultural barriers to consider?) |
| **Why?** | **Why** has this idea been developed? Why should we pay any attention to it? |
| **When?** | **When** did the idea originate, and is it still valid? When is the idea applicable/not applicable? When would it be reasonable or unreasonable to apply the idea? |
| **How?** | **How** will the idea work in practice? How can the idea be introduced? How are people likely to react? How will the idea be evaluated? How will we know or recognize success? |

## Chapter summary: Key learning points

- Understand that different people have different approaches and orientations towards their learning.
- Be aware of what your own learning orientations are – i.e. what makes you more likely to learn well and feel motivated.
- Use this self-awareness to guide your study plans and activities.
- Recognize that some learning and study techniques will work very well for you – it might take more time and practice to get used to others.
- Find out what techniques work best for you: get plenty of practice and remember to keep on looking for feedback about how you are doing.

### Suggested further reading

Gardner, H. (1999) *Intelligence Reframed: Multiple Intelligences for the 21st Century*. New York: Basic Books.

Gardner, H. (2006) *Multiple Intelligences: New Horizons in Theory and Practice*. New York: Basic Books.

Rose, C. (2000) *Master It Faster: How to Learn Faster, Make Good Decisions, and Think Creatively*. London: The Industrial Society.

# 4

# Taking It In and Working It Out: Ideas for reading, listening, making notes and critically thinking about information

## Chapter Contents

## Chapter Overview

- Developing ideas about listening effectively, reading well and thinking critically
- Using focused tips for remembering and recalling
- Practising active listening
- Extracting clarity and precision from learning material

## Introduction

This chapter will help you to focus on aspects of your learning that are often taken for granted in college and university. It is often assumed that you know how (and are motivated) to listen actively, to read extensively, to take useful notes during formal sessions, all the time remembering to think cleverly about the things you are trying to learn. The truth is often quite different. You may find yourself sitting absentmindedly in lectures or tutorials and at the end of it all, wondering what on earth it was about. You can start to feel vaguely worried about what you might have missed. You may be unsure about how to go about reading, how much of it you should be doing, and whether it is going to have any impact on your learning and performance as a student. When taking notes, it can be difficult to know what to write, and how to structure this. And, probably most importantly, it may be difficult to know how to lodge all this apparently important information firmly in your head so that you can use it effectively and think about it critically in a range of different ways.

This chapter will provide a framework that will help you to question, think critically about, interrogate and explore in analytical ways any of the material you encounter while you are learning. It emphasizes that one of the great habits to adopt, in education and in life, is not to take everything at face value. It will help you to consider the best way to take in information and ideas, but it will also encourage you to 'get underneath' information in a way that will assist you to bring judgement and wisdom of your own, and to apply that judgement to the information, ideas and claims that are out there.

## An exercise in listening, reading, making notes and memorizing

This section uses the actions of listening, reading, making notes and memorizing to help you to recognize the differences between deep and surface learning, and also show how even during a brief session like the one below, it is possible to engage with material at many different levels.

Ask someone to read the following passage to you and listen carefully to what the person is saying. Do not take notes while listening – just try as hard as you can to listen carefully to the person reading the passage and notice aspects of the message. Please do not read the passage yourself – have someone do this for you and listen as actively as you can.

---

*Exercise 4.1: Supper – by Nigella Lawson*

One of the oft-cited laments of those who don't really enjoy cooking is that a meal takes so much less time to eat than to cook. I don't mind that, not least because I always relish a bit of pottering about in the kitchen: it's the only time I ever get to myself. But also, I confess to an affinity with that Victorian worldview, the constant harping on the inevitability of decline – 'the woods decay, the woods decay and fall' that sort of thing – and the reminders that all things go back into the earth or up to the heavens. I don't resist the implacable cycle of meals, the kitchen grind.

Luckily, enough of my life is spent on what feels like some sort of cake-walk treadmill for me to have sympathy with those who have a less sentimental attachment to both the kitchen and my fond futilism. There are days, and probably those days are in the majority, when I feel I have no more than 10 minutes to get supper on the table. Yes, I am willing every now and then to have bread and cheese. I love bread and cheese. But most days I want a proper supper. And I mean 'proper'. I am not interested in making something easy but dispiriting to eat: as far as I'm concerned, every eating opportunity has to be relished, and the idea of wasting one by eating something I don't really want or that doesn't give me pleasure is too hideous to contemplate. It happens, but I am inconsolable afterwards.

Actually, I eat so fast that I'd have thought it would be impossible for me ever to find any recipe that takes less time to cook than to eat, but desperate times call for desperate measures – and if an exhausted weeknight, after a six o'clock meeting, a row over homework and a reproachful list of unreturned phone calls and emails doesn't call count as desperate times, I don't know what does. I need food I can cook fast or else – not least – I'll eat too much while I'm waiting for supper to be ready. Cook, feed thyself. And indeed I do. These are recipes that are almost too bare bones to be called that, using ingredients that need at most a quick blitz in a hot pan or a basic, effortless warm through. They're my fast fall-backs, the sort of meals I can cook when I'm squeezed for time at every angle. In other words, you can do a supermarket sweep at lunch and snatch yourself supper in the evening. And what's more, the washing up's minimal too'.

How much of this do you think you have taken in? In the space below, try to write the key points and issues that you remember. Give yourself about two minutes to try to remember the contents of the reading:

- How did you do?

- What parts of the reading were you best able to remember and were you able to focus on some pieces more than others?

- What main messages did you recall?

- Did you find it easy or did you struggle?

Practising your approach to listening and taking in information of any kind (even if it's Nigella Lawson's reflections on cooking) can help you to develop your approach to learning information that is associated with your studies.

Now compare what you remembered to the content of the passage and give yourself one of the following four grades: A, B, C or D.

A – Almost total recall: I remembered everything about this passage and was able to reproduce it accurately in my own words.

B – Good recall: I remembered at least 8 key points contained in the reading, and was able to articulate these points without much effort.

C – Some recall: I remembered some of what the passage contained and was able to write down at least 3–5 points contained in the reading.

D – Poor recall: I found it very difficult to remember much about what this passage contained.

What grade did you give yourself? If you scored an A or a B, then it is likely that you have already developed good basic skills in focusing on and absorbing information – you probably attended actively while you were listening to the passage and attempted to organize these ideas carefully and effectively enough to be able to reproduce and rearticulate those ideas in your own words.

You may have been more struck by some aspects of the messages contained in the passage than others and as a result you were probably able to remember those striking parts of the message more easily. Even if you did very well indeed, you will probably notice if you read over the passage yourself, that there were still key parts of the passage that you missed or were unable to recall. If you gave yourself a score of C or D, then do not worry too much – your ability to listen, focus and recall can very easily be improved. Very few people have perfect recall, but there are some relatively easy techniques you can use to improve your ability to take in and to remember a lot of information.

Some of these techniques have to do with concentration and focus, and others have to do with creating structures for yourself in order to organize and make coherent the information you are trying to absorb and understand.

Now go back to the passage and this time read it yourself. This time, plan to look for the answers to the following questions:

1   What is the **underlying message** in this reading? Are there several messages? Which do you think is the most important one?
2   How much of the reading simply outlines **one individual's opinion**? **How valid do you think that opinion is** based on what you know about the person who has written the piece?
3   Was there **anything that you disagreed with** in the passage? If so, **on what basis did you disagree**?
4   Was there anything **you did not understand** (a word or a reference or an argument)? If so, **what is the nature of that misunderstanding and how could you try to address it?** e.g. do you know what the words 'futilism' or 'dispiriting' mean? Can you guess what they might mean in the context of the text? Could you find out what those words mean and if you did, would it shed some more light on the part of the reading in which those words appear?
5   Are there any **critical insights you can bring to the passage?** What positive or negative assumptions has the writer adopted? (see also more about responding critically to texts later in this chapter).

Listening or reading that is guided by focused questions like the ones we have briefly outlined in Exercise 4.1 immediately helps you to develop greater ownership of material, a stronger sense of what it means and a sounder grasp of the essential messages, key points, relevant ideas and underlying assumptions that any particular reading contains.

Using prompts to guide your studies can really assist you in your efforts to structure and to understand material on your own terms, in your own way, and when you are listening to your tutors and lecturers or reading a chapter, journal article or research paper.

---

## Key tip

Deciding in advance what your objectives are when you are listening to a tutor/lecturer or reading a piece of text can help to make your listening and your reading focused, effective and memorable.

---

The advantage of reading – compared to listening to a lecture or attending a tutorial – is that you can do it at your own pace. You get to decide how fast or how slow you want to work through the material. You can search through text in order to uncover particular answers, and you can pinpoint parts of the text that seem most important or most useful for your own purposes. You can revisit and refocus on various aspects of the reading as the main ideas or arguments become clearer to you.

---

## Mnemonics

**Mnemonics are simple memory aids for retaining basic lists of items, concepts or important sequences**

If you like playing with words, and/or scored highly on Linguistic Intelligence (see Chapter 3), you may enjoy making up mnemonics to help you remember basic lists or key concepts. You use the first letter of each word you need to remember, to make a memorable phrase.

A well-known one to help remember the order of the planets, starting from closest to the sun to furthest (and including the now-relegated Pluto) is:

***My Very Educated Mother Just Served Us Nine Pizzas***

This stands for Mercury, Venus, Earth, Mars, Jupiter, Saturn, Uranus, Neptune and Pluto.

---

> **Key tip**
>
> Remember there is a difference between **taking notes** and **making notes**.
>
> Keep in mind that it is generally not useful to write down exactly what is contained in a text or to transcribe word for word what a tutor or lecturer says. This way of taking notes is a pretty passive activity and involves parroting what other people have written or said. A better strategy/orientation is to commit to 'making notes' – which is an active way of selecting, condensing, highlighting, structuring or paraphrasing the ideas and statements of other people.

### Reading for clarity, precision, relevance and other important characteristics

Some material that you read while studying is going to be accessible and easy to understand. Other material is likely to be complex and intricate. Some of it is going to make sense to you, but it is likely that you will encounter material that seems, at least at first, impossible to understand. It is up to you to figure out whether something you read is valuable or not. As you become more experienced, this will be easier to do, but initially students often find it difficult to differentiate between readings that will really add value to their learning, and those that will not.

Try to identify certain characteristics associated with the way a particular piece has been written. It helps to have a sense of the features of different kinds of readings and texts. Not all texts are equally valuable and you should be prepared to evaluate the readings you have been given based on a range of criteria.

Here is a list of the characteristics of text (see also Paul 1990). You should try to evaluate the information you are reading and learning based on the following kinds of features: clarity, precision, specificity, accuracy, relevance, consistency, logic, depth, completeness, significance, balance and adequacy. To do this, you need to be clear yourself what those words mean. Generate your own definitions of these terms and characteristics in the spaces below:

| **Clear** | **Unclear** |
|---|---|
| When an argument is clear it is | When an argument is unclear it is |
| | |

| | |
|---|---|
| **Precise**<br><br>When language is precise it is | **Imprecise**<br><br>When language is imprecise it is |
| **Specific**<br><br>When conclusions are specific they | **Vague**<br><br>When conclusions are vague they |
| **Accurate**<br><br>When information is accurate it is | **Inaccurate**<br><br>When information is inaccurate it is |
| **Relevant**<br><br>When arguments or data are relevant they are | **Irrelevant**<br><br>When arguments or data are irrelevant they are |
| **Consistent**<br><br>When conclusions/findings/claims are consistent they are | **Inconsistent**<br><br>When conclusions/findings/claims are inconsistent they are |
| **Logical**<br><br>When assertions are logical they are | **Illogical**<br><br>When assertions are illogical they are |

> **Key tip**
>
> When making notes, look out for key signals and prompts.
>
> Do not try to write everything down.
>
> Make notes in order to
>
> - **summarize,**
> - **question,**
> - **capture,**
> - **prompt**
> - **and highlight** key aspects of what you are taking in.
>
> Remember that it is also useful sometimes to put down your pen and just listen.

Active note making remains an important skill in higher education. There is a lot of evidence suggesting that nowadays students make fewer notes, and are more likely to rely on web-based information and resources supplied by or recommended by their teachers as a substitute for note making (Moore and Murphy 2005). However, the benefits of note making are more wide-reaching than the pragmatic value associated with keeping a record. Good note making helps you to learn material in ways that might otherwise be more difficult.

### Listening and the positive effects of body language

Carry out your own research experiment on the possible impact of student body language.

Observe the behaviour of most of the students in your class and try to trace any possible impact of student behaviour on your teacher's orientation. What key lessons does this suggest to you? Write down the conclusions of this study and the implications for your own behaviour and body language as a student.

1 Over a period of two weeks, note down some of the most noticeable features of students' body language in class (e.g. looking out of window, talking to other students during a demonstration, smiling, frowning, nodding). Is the body language largely positive or negative? What are your reasons for coming to a 'positive' or 'negative' evaluation of student body language?
2 Interpret this body language and try to infer from the body language what messages are being sent to the teacher.
3 Observe the skills and activities of the teacher and try to see if you can find any direct links between student behaviour and teacher effectiveness.
4 Based on these observations generate your own list of 'do's and don'ts' for student body language in class.

When you listen authentically and respectfully to other people, you automatically increase the likelihood that they will communicate effectively in your company. In a classic piece of research by Susan Klein (1971), it was shown that when students smile, look attentive, attempt to answer questions and appear engaged, then teachers respond more positively and helpfully. You can affect how good your teachers are. You can impact on their commitment and their willingness to help you learn. Good listening is an important starting point for having such an influence. Do not underestimate the power you have to give rise to positive responses from those around you.

## The importance of the reading habit

Like many skills, your capacity to read becomes sharper and better the more you practise it. The more you read, and the more you engage with complicated texts of all kinds, the more likely it will be that you will find it easier to stay on top of your course material and to get through your reading lists. Reading for pleasure, reading novels and newspapers, reading for understanding and reading for practice will help you to become better at using texts to develop your learning. If you do not read a lot outside of your course of study, it may be difficult for you to keep up when course work and readings are being assigned. Getting into the habit of reading is an important thing to do as you work to become a more able and accomplished student.

### *Developing your reading habit*

Here are some suggestions for developing and enhancing your reading habit:

- Join a **book club** (or set up your own).
- Read together with other people in **groups and see what different interpretations people often bring to the same reading**.
- **Distribute different reading tasks** in study groups and focus your group meetings **on discussing, exploring and summarizing** what each member has read.
- Become a **versatile reader – read many different types and forms** of text to sharpen and enhance your reading skills.
- Develop the habit of **reading every day**.

And remember: **practise reading to prompts**, e.g. what is the main point of this? If someone asked me to write a 200 word summary of this piece of text, what essential information would I include? How does this compare to other material I have read? What other things should I read now that I have read this?

### Generating your listening, reading, note–making and memorizing strategies by asking the right questions

The spoken word is very temporary and difficult to pin down, but there are all sorts of advantages of listening to an expert on a topic (see also Chapter 2) that make listening an important activity and something you can become more skilled in. Also, it is not just experts that you should listen to – listening to fellow students' interpretations and ideas can also develop and enhance your understanding. Pay attention to the speaker, try not to get distracted. Use any opportunity you have to clarify what the person is saying, and use clarification questions to make sure that you understand the most important aspects.

### *Reading more effectively*

You may find it will be easier to avoid procrastination and distraction if you read for short, concentrated periods of time and make your reading as **active** as possible. You could try the approach described in the diagram.

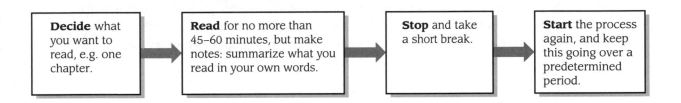

| **Decide** what you want to read, e.g. one chapter. | **Read** for no more than 45–60 minutes, but make notes: summarize what you read in your own words. | **Stop** and take a short break. | **Start** the process again, and keep this going over a predetermined period. |

Browne and Keeley (2007) suggest posing questions that can help you to read, listen and think in constructively critical ways. Use them as you are grappling with a chapter or a research paper or reading on your course.

### *What are the reasons for the conclusions?*

There are a lot of possible reasons why certain people or groups come to certain conclusions about an issue – not all of these conclusions are necessarily valid. (Remember that tobacco companies used to tell everyone that smoking was safe – think about why they used to do that and how other information can be distorted for similar kinds of reasons.) There are other reasons why people draw false conclusions: if someone is lecturing to a group and they have already publicly stated a position on something, it is harder for them to back down, even when evidence is presented that undermines what they have said.

The point is that seemingly authoritative speakers and writers do not always get things right. Sometimes they draw the wrong conclusions by mistake. Other times they do it on purpose – presenting the wrong conclusions because it is in their interests to do so. You need to be aware that sometimes the truth can be obscured because of people's own blind spots or because of their motives. If you are going to bring yourself critically to the activities of reading or listening, always keep this in mind.

*Which words or phrases are ambiguous?*

Underline every word or phrase that you do not understand, and arm yourself with a dictionary and or a thesaurus or even better, a specialist dictionary that focuses on words and phrases within your discipline. (There are dictionaries of medicine, of economics, of sociology of history, of research methodology among many others, and they contain specialist vocabulary that can help you to navigate your way through material that in the early days of your studies may seem impossible to understand.) If you commit to 'translating' text or lectures that seem terribly obscure and difficult, you will very quickly learn to gain clarity and comfort with even the most awkward and complex texts. Academic disciplines do sometimes express their ideas in quite stylized and intricate ways. One of your first reading/listening tools will be to translate this into a language that you are comfortable with. Over time, you will get more and more used to understanding and tackling lots of different kinds of texts. Clarifying ambiguous words and phrases can be a real help from the very start of your time at college or university.

**Digging deeper**

Why should you believe your teachers and lecturers? Because they are more expert than you are? Because they have carried out research in the area that you are studying? Because they set the assessment and correct it? None of these are good reasons to accept things at face value. If you are going to become an active, effective learner, then it pays not to take anything for granted. When Michael Shermer (a leading American scientist) is asked by his students why they should believe him, he replies that they shouldn't! The point is that your journey at university should be about working on becoming an investigative, self-directed, empowered learner. You need to check things out for yourself or at least to ask as many questions as possible that will help you get to the bottom of any claim that is made inside or indeed outside of a classroom.

*More critical questions for digging deeper*

**How reliable** *is the source of the claim?*

You can check this question by finding out how much research a particular author has carried out on the subject they are discussing, what is known about their work, and how reliable their work is considered to be by independent commentators.

**Have the claims been verified** *by another separate source?*

Again, a review of research within a particular area should be able to tell you more about the nature of a particular claim about how much weight other investigators apply to the strength of the arguments made.

**How does the claim fit with other knowledge** *about how the world works?*

Compare someone's claim to what you already know or think about the way the world works. Sometimes your own common sense might make you doubt a particular claim. Perhaps your common sense is wrong, but it may also be that the claim is – consider and explore and try to verify the claims in a number of ways before accepting or rejecting them.

*Has anyone gone out of their way to* **disprove the claim***, or has only supportive evidence been sought?*

Some truisms become so embedded in the way people think that few ever seek to question or challenge those so-called truths. Keep in mind that there was a time when everyone assumed that the world was flat. There was a time when people didn't think smoking was bad for your health. There was a time when doctors didn't think there was any need to wash their hands before or after attending to a patient. It's only when people dedicate themselves to disproving assumptions, that those assumptions get put to the test. Putting assumptions to the test is a good way of staying on top of your learning in a way that is critical, intelligent and engaged. It's a good habit to get into when you're learning and studying at university.

*Is there* **other evidence out there that points to a different conclusion** *or counterclaim?*

Search for other evidence; talk to people about the claims or conclusions you are learning about. See if there are perspectives, insights, ideas and evidence out there to point to or at least to suggest other alternatives. Doing this will make your learning of your subject more robust and ultimately more motivating.

(Adapted from Shermer 1997)

---

### Chapter summary: Key learning points

Education is not the filling of a bucket but the lighting of a fire.

(W.B. Yeats)

- Don't just commit to covering the material on your programme of study.
- Ask questions and interrogate texts and tutors.
- Practise critical reading.
- Explore the logic (or otherwise) of what you are being asked to learn.
- Relate what you are learning to other things that you have learned.
- Test what you have learned in other contexts or by gathering more evidence and perspectives.
- Apply the principles of active reading and critical thinking to the note making techniques you saw in Chapter 3.

---

### Suggested further reading

Hughes, W. and Lavery, J. (2008) *Critical Thinking: An Introduction to the Basic Skills*, 5th edn. Peterborough, Ont.: Broadview Press.

# Research Skills and Orientations: First steps to good research

## 5

## Chapter Contents

## Chapter Overview

- **Defining research**
- **Introducing research activities and orientations**
- **Understanding the purpose of literature reviews and practical exercises for doing them**
- **Discovering useful information about research methods**
- **Learning about research pitfalls and how to avoid them**

## Introduction

**Research is** a process of inquiry and investigation which can help to solve practical problems and increase knowledge. Research can be one of the most absorbing features of any degree course, as it offers you a fair measure of control and independence over what you learn. It also gives you an opportunity to confirm, clarify, pursue – or even discover – new aspects or perspectives on a chosen topic. You can become a person who contributes knowledge to society. Research can give you a chance to take a subject that really interests you, formulate questions about the topic, and pursue answers, or explore new perspectives to these questions in a way that advances knowledge about the research subject a little (or sometimes a lot) further.

Research will also draw together skills you have developed, both inside and outside of higher education, including information retrieval; social skills; writing skills; and presentation skills. Your research project is likely to carry with it a significant percentage of your course marks – so it is an important contributor to your overall degree grade.

This chapter offers an introduction to research and research methods and assumes that you are beginning to think about a research topic at either undergraduate or postgraduate level. The chapter also considers ethical issues, research methodology and common research problems.

In addition to the information presented in the chapter, there are two types of activity we hope you will engage with:

- **Personal research activities** will ask you to think about the research topic that interests you and what you hope to achieve.
- **Exercises will** encourage and help you to think about the issues underpinning a particular topic. There are 14 exercises in the chapter.

## The purpose of research

Research involves one or more of the following:

- Reviewing, contributing to, or synthesizing existing knowledge.
- Testing ideas, models and theories.
- Investigating existing situations or problems.
- Exploring and analysing current or past events, situations or phenomena.
- Providing interpretations or solutions to existing problems.
- Generating new knowledge.
- Explaining a new phenomena.
- Constructing or creating new procedures or systems.

> (Collis and Hussey, Business Research: A Practical Guide for Undergraduate and Postgraduate Students, reproduced with permission of Palgrave Macmillan)

### *Originality and research*

Ground-breaking and completely original research is very uncommon for the type of research you are likely to be doing. However, the specific research questions that you pursue, the setting for your research, the way you gather and present your information can offer opportunities for some originality. This is one of the purposes of the literature review (see next section): to help you to identify what has been done before, and how. This can guide you towards different approaches in your own research.

*Personal research activity: your research interest*

 What is the **main aim** of your research? Write one or two sentences that summarize the overall aim of your research project.

Now identify up to three **specific research questions** that flow from this main research aim.

**Question 1**

**Question 2**

**Question 3**

You are likely to be involved in only a small-scale research project, so you should aim to generate a manageable number of research questions. If you have more than three questions in mind, we suggest you discuss your research project idea with your supervisor.

*Personal research activity: background to your research interest*

What is the background to your interest in this topic area? **Why** have you chosen this area for research? Summarize briefly the reasons why this topic is of interest to you.

We will return to your research interests later in this chapter.

### The literature review: background and preparatory reading

The literature review is an essential stage of the research process, for the following reasons:

- It is essential you know what previous studies have been done in your chosen topic area. There is no point in spending time to produce a research finding and outcome identical to another.
- It will help you learn more about the existing ideas and theories in your chosen topic area.
- As stated earlier, understanding what has been done before will help you to identify new or different research approach possibilities in your chosen topic.
- It will help you to justify your research topic to your supervisor/tutor at the project proposal stage.

---

*Personal research activity: checklist for reviewing previous studies*   ☑

A checklist for reviewing previous studies, and for helping to determine your own research approach, has been suggested by Collis and Hussey (2003). You could use it for your own research planning purposes. Take a previous study and ask the following questions of it.

☐ What was the **purpose** of the previous study? How does it differ from other studies I have encountered and my own research ideas?

☐ What **methodology** was used in the previous study? How does it differ from my own proposed research? (The term 'methodology' is discussed later in this chapter, but generally refers to how the research was conducted, including the means used to gather data.)

☐ What were the **findings** in the study; how do they differ from other studies and what I expect to find?

☐ What were the **limitations and weaknesses** of the study? (Often the researcher(s) will highlight these in the 'Discussion' sections of their reports.)

*Exercise 5.1: Finding sources*

There may be a mass of information available – or very little – on your proposed research topic. How can you get started? How can you begin to find relevant sources?

Here are some starting points:

- Ask your supervisor or other tutors for suggestions.
- Look at the bibliographies of peer-reviewed journal articles written on the topic for other relevant sources.

**What else could you do to find relevant sources**? Write in the space below other ways you could begin to identify relevant sources.

See the end of this chapter for our comments (p. 87).

### Primary and secondary sources

The selection of relevant material – but of the right quality – is an essential component in conducting a literature review. If faced with a mass of information on a topic, how can you begin to discriminate and choose which sources to use? You may, for example, get sidetracked into using secondary sources, when you should be using those with a more primary role to play in supporting evidence.

- *Primary sources*: evidence that comes **directly from** the people, the time, the place, the agencies involved in the event or phenomenon in question.
- *Secondary sources*: material produced **about** the event or phenomenon, or the commentary or interpretation of others about theories, models, ideas, definitions and practices.

---

**Key tip**

**Primary** source material should be used for your central definitions, main descriptions, quotations, key points, arguments and assertions.

**Secondary** source material should be used for lesser definitions, factual information, illustrative examples and supporting points.

---

**Exercise 5.2: *Identifying primary and secondary sources***

| What primary sources can you think of? Write in the space below. | What secondary sources can you think of? Write in the space below. |
|---|---|
|  |  |

See the end of this chapter for our comments (p. 87–88).

### Choosing sources

For both electronic and printed sources there are essentially three cascading areas of inquiry to help you select the best sources (see Figure 5.1).

The first two will help you to determine which sources to choose if more than one appears relevant to the point you are making.

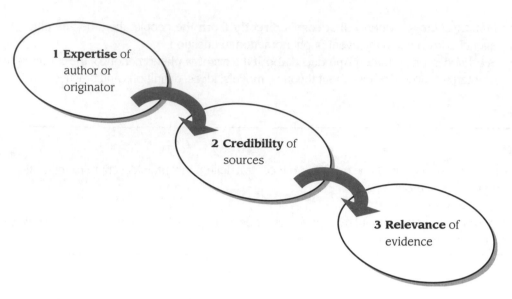

Figure 5.1 **Three cascading areas of inquiry**

### *Expertise of author or originator*

In relation to **expertise** of author or originator, you can ask the following general questions of both printed and electronic sources:

- What qualifications and experience does the author/originator have?
- Is the author well known in his or her field?
- What else has the author published?
- Is the author published by a well-known publishing house? or peer reviewed journals?
- Do other writers in the field of study refer to this author in their work?
- Do your tutors mention this author?

You can ask further questions specifically for electronic sources:

- Is the site managed by the author?
- If not, is it clear who is taking 'ownership' of the online information presented?
- Is there a link to any named author's email address?

### *Credibility of sources*

Exercise 5.3 asks you to think about questions for determining the credibility of sources.

---

*Exercise 5.3: **What questions could you ask to determine the credibility of a source?***

| What general questions could you ask to determine the credibility of a source? Write in the space below. | What questions specifically about electronic sources could you ask? Write in the space below. |
|---|---|
|  |  |

See the end of this chapter for our comments (p. 88).

---

## Different categories of research

There are four main categories of research: exploratory, descriptive, analytical and predictive (Collis and Hussey 2003).

- **Exploratory research** is undertaken when few or no previous studies exist in the topic area. The aim is to look for patterns, hypotheses or ideas that can be advanced tentatively and will form the basis for further research.
- **Descriptive research** can be used to identify and classify the elements or characteristics of the subject. This type of research is particularly useful when you need to look closely at the **what** features of a topic, for example, what is happening; what are the component parts or features of the subject.

- **Analytical research** often extends the descriptive approach to suggest or explain **why** or **how** something is happening, for example the underlying causes of a particular situation. An important feature of this type of research is the process of locating and identifying the different factors (or variables) involved.
- **Predictive research** enables you to speculate intelligently on future possibilities, based on a close analysis of available cause and effect evidence.

(Adapted from Collis and Hussey 2003)

## Ethical issues and research

Ethics concerns the system of moral principles by which individuals can judge their own actions, and the actions of others, as right or wrong, good or bad.

Ethical concerns and questions may emerge at all stages of research. However, there may not always be clear-cut answers, as the case study exercise will show. Nevertheless, it is important that researchers consider seriously the ethical boundaries, research processes, and implications of their research.

You may have a clear idea what you want to achieve, but your research may involve the feelings, lives, and even livelihoods of the people involved. The questions you ask – and the issues these may stir to the surface – can impact onto the lives of others. For example, the participants in your research may not agree with your interpretation or solution of a situation or a problem that affects them; their perspectives and views of the same situation may be entirely at odds with yours! So, ethical considerations are an important research issue – and you may, therefore, be required to submit your research proposal to a research ethics committee within your institution before you can proceed.

*Exercise 5.4: Ethical case study on store assistants*

You have been working for over a year in a local chain store as a part-time store assistant. You have observed that there is an undercurrent of tension and bad feeling in the store between staff members, so you are interested in studying more closely the ways staff relate to and communicate with each other. What ethical issues are you likely to be confronted with in this situation? Write in the space below.

See the end of this chapter for our comments (p. 89).

*Exercise 5.5: Seven ethical issues for researchers*

 Saunders et al. (2009) see the avoidance of harm to others as a 'cornerstone' of research. They suggest there are at least seven ethical issues that researchers need to consider and address. We have started you off with two of these. Can you think of others? Write in the spaces below.

1   Issues concerning the rights of privacy of individuals.

2   Issues concerning the voluntary nature of participation – and the rights of individuals to withdraw partially or completely from the process.

3   Issues concerning . . .

4   Issues concerning . . .

5   Issues concerning . . .

6   Issues concerning . . .

7   Issues concerning . . .

See the end of this chapter for our comments (p. 90).

### Four approaches to research

A research project can involve various approaches. In this context 'approaches' means the theoretical position you take on **how** a research topic is to be investigated. Four such approaches can be identified:

- **Deductive**.
- **Inductive**.
- **Positivistic**.
- **Phenomenological**.

> ### Key tip
>
> Don't be awed by the jargon of research. It is important you have a basic understanding of some of the key terms you will encounter; but don't let it intimidate you.

This section is about your **starting point** for the investigation of the research questions or issues you wish to pursue.

### Deductive approaches

Deductive research is when you start with a particular theory, model or idea in mind, and set out to test its validity in a particular situation, to see if the theory, model or practice 'fits' or connects with it.

### Inductive approaches

Inductive research is where you start by looking closely at a particular situation, then identify the characteristics, elements or features of it. You then make or infer connections with available theories, models or ideas – or develop a new theory to explain it.

### Positivistic approaches

Positivistic approaches to research are characterized by a detached, often quantitative (or measurable) way of researching to seek in a systematic way the facts or causes of any phenomena.

Positivistic approaches seek to identify, measure, and evaluate phenomena and to provide a rational explanation for them.

This explanation will often attempt to establish causal links and relationships between the different elements (or variables) of the subject, and relate them to a particular theory or practice.

This type of research, although harder to design initially, is usually highly detailed and structured; results can be collated easily and presented statistically.

### Phenomenological approaches

Phenomenological (or qualitative) approaches start from a position that some phenomena are not easily 'measured'. Human motivation, for example, is inconsistent and shaped by factors not always observable; therefore it can be difficult to generalize on motivation from the measured observation of behaviour alone.

This phenomenological perspective also accepts the premise that people will often influence events and can act in unpredictable ways that go against rules or norms; metaphorically, they are often 'actors' on a human stage and shape their 'performance' in response to a wide range of variables.

Research methods are chosen, therefore, to try and describe, translate, explain, or **interpret** events from the perspectives of the people involved in the research.

### Combining approaches

Research projects can often involve **a combination of approaches**. For example, deductive research can often identify new phenomena and patterns in the data that lead the researchers to develop new theories, models, or ideas. And research that may be significantly biased towards positivistic/quantitative approaches may also contain more subjective phenomenological/ qualitative elements. You can, however, indicate in your research proposal your **starting position**, for example, a deductive approach to the topic.

### Research methodology

Why do you need to think so carefully about research approaches? The reason is that your research approach will impact on the **methodology** you adopt. The term **methodology** refers to the broad, overall approaches and perspectives to the research process, and is concerned with the following main issues:

- **Why** and how you collected certain data.
- **What** data you collected.
- **Where** you collected the data.
- **How** you collated and analysed the data.

Research methods specifically refer to the various specific tools or ways data can be collected and analysed – for example your sampling techniques, the questionnaires you produce, or the interview or observation checklists used in the study. Research methods are described in the section starting on p. 68.

Two main research methodologies are positivistic and phenomenological approaches. However, as suggested earlier, research may combine approaches, so your research may contain **both** positivistic and phenomenological elements; for example a qualitative survey of data could also contain researcher impressions gained from observation.

Positivistic approaches include the following:

- Surveys.
- Experimental studies.
- Longitudinal studies.
- Cross-sectional studies.

Phenomenological approaches include the following:

- Case studies.
- Action research.
- Observation.
- Participative inquiry.

## *Positivistic methodologies*

### *Surveys*

Surveys involve selecting a sample of subjects drawn from the group you wish to study. The main methods of asking questions are by face-to-face or telephone interviews, by using questionnaires, or a mixture of both.

There are two main types of survey – but again, combined approaches are possible:

- **Descriptive** survey, concerned with identifying and counting the frequency of a particular response among the survey group.
- **Analytical** survey, to analyse the relationship between different elements (variables) in a sample group.

There is more detail later in this chapter about surveys (see under 'Research methods').

### *Experimental studies*

Experimental studies are done in controlled and structured environments and enable the causal relationships of phenomena to be identified and analysed.

The variables can be manipulated or controlled to observe the effects on the subjects studied. For example, sound, light, or heat can be managed to observe the effects.

Studies done in laboratories, or other controlled environments, tend to offer the best opportunities for controlling the variables in a rigorous way, although when human subjects are involved the artificiality of the situation can affect the responses of the people studied.

*Longitudinal studies*

Longitudinal studies are done over an extended period to observe the effect that time has on the situation under observation, and to collect data of these changes. Longitudinal studies are often conducted over several years, which make them unsuitable for most relatively short taught undergraduate or postgraduate courses.

However, it is possible to base short timescale research on primary data collected by others in longitudinal studies, for example government agencies, and then to subject one or more aspects or elements of it to your own close analysis.

*Cross-sectional studies*

Cross-sectional studies are done when time or resources for more extended research are limited. They involve close analysis of a situation at a chosen point in time, to give a 'snapshot' result. You might look at the similarities or differences between people in one or more organizations, for instance, the information technology skills of managers in a number of companies.

## *Phenomenological methodologies*

*Case studies*

A case study offers an opportunity to study a subject in depth, and usually involves gathering and analysing information; this information may be both qualitative and quantitative. Case studies can be used to formulate theories, or be:

- **Descriptive**: for example, where current practice is described in detail.
- **Illustrative**: for example, where the case studies illustrate new practices adopted by an organization.
- **Exploratory**: for example, where you explore the cause and effect of a particular situation or phenomenon.
- **Explanatory**: for example, where theories are used as a basis for understanding, informing, or explaining practices or procedures.

*Action research*

Action research involves an intervention by a researcher to influence change in any given situation; the researcher will then monitor and evaluate the results. For example, the researcher, working with a particular company, aims to improve the company's telephone responses to customers, and explores ways this might be done. The researcher might introduce new techniques and monitors the results. However, this research requires active cooperation between researcher and the company concerned and a continual process of adjustment to the intervention, based on responses from both the employees of the company and their customers.

*Observation*

Observation research evolved from anthropology and the close study of societies. **Participant observation** is where the researcher becomes a working member of the group or situation to be observed. The aim is to understand the situation from the inside: from the viewpoints and experiences of the people in the situation. This form of research can be particularly effective in the study of small groups.

Participant observation can be **overt**, when everyone knows it is happening, or **covert**, when the subject(s) being observed for research purposes are **unaware** it is happening. In covert observation, you need to think about what ethical issues might be raised with and by this approach (see section on 'Ethical issues and research').

*Participative inquiry*

Participative inquiry is about research within one's own group or organization and involves the active participation and cooperation of people you would normally work, study or associate with on a daily basis. You would try to involve the whole group in the research and you would make the research process as open and transparent as possible to all. As you can imagine, this type of research can work effectively only where the researcher is an active and known member of any group.

*Exercise 5.6:  What do you think are the main advantages/positives and disadvantages/negatives of both positivistic and phenomenological approaches in research?*

Write in the two grids that follow: Positivistic and Phenomenological.

**Positivistic**

| Advantages / Positives | Disadvantages / Negatives |
| --- | --- |
| | |

**Phenomenological**

| Advantages / Positives | Disadvantages / Negatives |
| --- | --- |
| | |

See the end of this chapter for our comments (p. 90).

---

*Personal research activity: your research approach and methodology*

At the beginning of this chapter you were asked to summarize the topic of research that interested you. Now try to clarify what **approach** and **methodology** would suit the type of research you have in mind. Try also to think of a title that encapsulates what the research is about. Write in the space below.

| **Title**<br>(Think of a title that describes succinctly the nature of your proposed research) | **Your approach**<br>(for example, positivistic/ phenomenological; deductive/inductive) | **Your methodology**<br>(for example, case study, survey, cross-sectional studies) |
| --- | --- | --- |
| | | |

---

### Research methods

Methodology is about the **broad approach** you will take to your research, and research methods are about the **tools or the specific means** that you will use to collect your data. The data can be secondary or primary:

- **Secondary** data are produced by others that you use for your research purposes.
- **Primary** data are produced by you in the course of your research.

### *Sampling*

Before you start any research involving other people, you need to think about **sampling**. This means how you will go about choosing or finding the target number of people to be involved in your research for the purposes of data collection. It is often necessary to look for ways of gathering data from a representative number of people from any group rather than from them all, although in a positivistic study, when seeking the views of a group of 50 or less, Henry (1990) argues against any form of sampling. He argues that you should distribute questionnaires to and collect data from the entire population, if possible.

However, to elicit the views of larger groups some form of sampling is usually necessary, particularly in the type of small-scale research you are likely to be involved in. Sampling strategies are divided into two main groups: probability and non-probability sampling.

## Probability sampling

Probability sampling is where the researcher has a significant measure of control over who is selected and on the selection methods. Main methods of probability sampling are as follows:

- **Simple random sampling**: selection at random by the researchers from a choice of subjects.
- **Systematic sampling**: selection by the researchers at numbered intervals; for example, every one person in five in the target group.
- **Stratified sampling**: sampling within particular sections of the target groups; for example, you target a specific number of people based on the percentage of the total group that share the same characteristics. So, for instance, in a study of an organization that had 50 managers and 800 machinists, a 10 per cent representative sample of this population would involve 5 managers and 80 machinists.
- **Cluster sampling**: surveying particular clusters of subjects that share naturally occurring groupings; for example, groups of companies classified by product or area.

## Non-probability sampling

Non-probability sampling is where the researcher has little initial control over the choice of subject for selection, or where controlled selection of participants is not a critical factor. Main methods of non-probability sampling are as follows:

- **Convenience sampling**: sampling those subjects in a way most convenient to the researcher.
- **Voluntary sampling**: the participants are self-selecting; they come forward voluntarily in response to an appeal.
- **Purposive sampling**: enables you to use your judgement to choose people from those presented or available that best meet your research objectives.
- **'Snowball' sampling**: starts with one person, who then suggests another, and so on.
- **Event sampling**: uses the opportunity presented by a particular event, for example, a conference, to make contacts with likely research subjects.
- **Time sampling**: involves recognizing that different times or days of the week or year may be significant, and sampling takes place at these times or days.

---

### Exercise 5.7: What sampling strategy was used in this study?

In the early 1990s a study examined the personal characteristics of 50 highly successful independent retailers. The 50 were contacted through business networks across England. The names of potential respondents were passed to the researchers by the chairs of these networks. The researchers wrote to the retailers concerned and invited them to participate in the survey, which included the completion of a questionnaire and interview with the researcher.

See the end of this chapter for our answer (p. 91).

What sample size will you aim for? Which sampling method will you adopt? Say which, and why.

### Data gathering methods

Having decided on a sample size and broad sampling method, you can plan your approach to gathering data. There are three main ways of gathering data:

- Interviews.
- Questionnaires.
- Group discussions or focus groups.

### Interviews

Interviews can be grouped into three main types:

- **Structured.**
- **Semi-structured.**
- **Unstructured.**

*Structured interviews*

Structured interviews involve the use of questionnaires based on a predetermined and identical set of questions. The researcher usually reads the question in a neutral voice to a subject, to avoid influencing or prompting a particular response (see also the section on questionnaires).

*Semi-structured interviews*

When conducting a semi-structured interview, the interviewer will have a list of themes and areas to be covered and there may be some standardized questions, but the interviewer may omit, or add to, some of these, depending on the situation and the flow of the conversation.

*Unstructured interviews*

Unstructured interviews are informal discussions where the interviewer wants to explore a topic in a spontaneous but in-depth way with another person. However, even in unstructured interviews it is likely that the researcher would have a pre-decided range of topics to cover in the discussion.

**Exercise 5.8: What types of research project might favour a structured interview approach? Write in the space below.**

**Exercise 5.9: What types of research project might favour a semi-structured or unstructured interview approach? Write in the space below.**

See the end of this chapter for our comments on both these exercises (p. 91).

### Interview problems

There are potential problem areas associated with interviews:

- Demeanour.
- Suspicion.
- Bias.
- Confidentiality.
- Conduct of interview.

### Demeanour

Generally speaking, we often like people who appear to like us. The interviewer should be interested in the interviewee, but in a neutral and pleasant way: 'neutrally interested' is the best way of describing an ideal interviewer–interviewee relationship. The tone of voice of the interviewer is important, as it should project an impression of quiet enthusiasm for the topic under discussion.

An open posture is also recommended: where the interviewer sits slightly forward towards the interviewee and keeps eye contact. The interviewer should avoid appearing shocked, disbelieving, or astonished by comments made by interviewees.

### Suspicion

People are increasingly suspicious of interviewers and their motives. Many people have experience of being stopped by interviewers who appear to be asking questions in a neutral way, but are really seeking to make marketing contacts for commercial organizations. The true purpose of the interview should be carefully explained to the interviewee and also how the data collected will be used. Ideally, the student researcher should have a letter from a tutor explaining the research, for example that it is part of an undergraduate or postgraduate course. In a scheduled interview the interviewer should send details of the process and agenda to interviewees in advance and explain, for example, the estimated length of time it will take, and the aim, purpose, and range of the proposed questions.

### Bias

Bias can affect the responses of the interviewer to interviewee, and vice versa. A range of factors can influence and colour our perceptions of the people we encounter. We can like or dislike someone, often without quite knowing why, and this can affect our responses to them. Why do you think that is?

*Exercise 5.10: How might bias affect the responses of the interviewer and interviewee? Write in the space below.*

See the end of this chapter for our comments (p. 91).

*Confidentiality*

As stated earlier, the issue of confidentiality is an important one. With interviews, interviewees may be worried about disclosing sensitive or personal information in case it has negative repercussions for them, or might be used to target them for marketing purposes.

Interviewees **must** be given complete reassurance about confidentiality and told who will see the data obtained, but do not forget that this is likely to include at least two university tutors, and possibly one external examiner.

The interviewee should be assured that his or her views will be anonymous and generalized in the final report, unless the interviewee wishes or agrees otherwise.

*Conduct of interview*

The opening stages of an interview are particularly important. Saunders et al. (2007) make the following suggestions on conducting a semi-structured interview:

- The interviewee is thanked for agreeing to the meeting.
- The purpose of the research, its funding (if relevant), and progress to date are briefly outlined.

- The interviewee is given an assurance regarding confidentiality.
- The interviewee's right not to answer questions is emphasized, and it is made clear the interviewee can terminate the discussion at any time.
- The interviewee is told about how it is proposed to use the data collected during and after the project.
- The interviewer describes the process of the interview, for example the approximate number and range of questions to be asked, and the time the interview is likely to take.

## Questionnaires

There are four types of questionnaire approaches:

- Questionnaire sent as an email attachment, preceded by an email message.
- Postal questionnaire, sent with an accompanying letter.
- Telephone contact first, then completion of questionnaire sent electronically or by post.
- Delivery and collection of printed questionnaires (for distribution by others), usually preceded or accompanied by an explanatory letter, telephone call or email.

Before you produce a questionnaire, you need to clarify what it is you want to learn and what data you need to obtain. You also need to think ahead about how you are going to **collate** the information you gather. There is no point in designing a questionnaire that produces a range of information which is difficult or impossible to collate. Wherever possible, questionnaires should be piloted with a small group to test the questionnaire for weaknesses.

The questions you ask others can be 'closed' or 'open' in nature, but should always be presented in a logical sequence.

### Closed questions

Closed questions are where a limited number of alternative responses to the set question are provided. These can be in list, category, ranking, scale/rating, grid or other quantitative form. They can be pre-coded on a questionnaire to facilitate analysis; for example 'Which brand do you prefer? Please rank the brands shown below with your fist, second, and third choices' or 'Please state which one of the following you prefer . . .'

### Open questions

Open questions involve posing a question but leaving space for the respondent's own answer; for example: 'In the space that follows please tell me which brand you prefer and why' or 'Please summarize in the spaces below your responses to each of the following . . .' The question in the exercise that follows uses an open question.

*Exercise 5.11: What do you think are the respective research advantages and disadvantages of asking open and closed questions? Write in the space below.*

**Open questions**

| Advantages | Disadvantages |
| --- | --- |
|  |  |

**Closed questions**

| Advantages | Disadvantages |
| --- | --- |
|  |  |

See the end of this chapter for our comments (p. 92).

*Some general rules for designing questionnaires*

- Explain the purpose of the questionnaire to all participants.
- Keep your questionnaire as **short** as possible, but include all the questions you need to cover.
- Keep your questions as **simple** as possible; avoid asking hypothetical questions unless you are sure the participants can cope with them.
- Do not use jargon or specialist language (unless you are sure that the participants really prefer and understand it).
- Phrase each question so that only one meaning is possible.
- Avoid ambiguous words, such as 'large' and 'small'.
- Avoid asking negative questions, as these are easy to misinterpret. If you have to ask these, for example on a survey of attitudes, try using a mixture of positive and negative questions.
- Ask only one question at a time.
- Include, if possible, questions which serve as cross-checks on the answers to other questions.
- Avoid leading or value-laden questions that might imply what the required answer might be.
- Avoid asking questions that might be construed as offensive or insensitive by the participants.
- Avoid asking 'difficult' questions, which the respondent might struggle to answer; for example, performing calculations or spelling words (people hate to look stupid by not knowing the 'answer').
- Always thank the respondents for answering the questions, and offer to keep them informed of your findings.

(Adapted from Blaxter et al. 2006).

*Examples of types of survey questions*

Specific information request

In which year did you start your current degree course? _____

Category

Have you ever been, or are you currently, a student representative? Tick which of the following applies to you.

**Yes** (currently) _____ **Yes** (in the past) _____ **No** (never) _____

Multiple choice

Do you view the money you have spent on your higher education as any of the following? If so, tick which.

A luxury _____ An investment _____ A necessity _____ A gamble _____ A burden _____

Other _____ Please give more details if you tick 'Other' _____

_____

Open questions (example)

Please summarize the benefits of your degree study in the space below:

_____

_____

Ranking

What do you see as the main purpose(s) of your degree study? Please rank all those relevant in order from 1 (most important) downwards:

Personal development _____ Career advancement _____ Subject interest _____

Recreation _____ Fulfil ambition _____ Intellectual stimulation _____

Other _____ Please give details of 'other' reasons in the space below:

_____

_____

Grid or table

How would you rank the benefits of your degree study for each of the following? Please rank each item by placing a cross in the relevant box.

| Benefits for . . . | Very positive | Positive | Neutral | Negative | Very negative | Not sure |
|---|---|---|---|---|---|---|
| You | | | | | | |
| Your family | | | | | | |
| Your employer | | | | | | |
| Your country | | | | | | |
| Your community | | | | | | |
| Your friends | | | | | | |

*Exercise 5.12: Scaling the responses to questions*

The following example shows how responses to questions can be scaled. However, what is the problem with the question posed below?

How would you describe your parents' attitude to higher education at the time you applied? Please tick one of the options below.

Very Positive _____ Positive _____ Mixed/Neutral _____ Negative _____
Very Negative _____ Not Sure _____

If you would like to add any comments about your response, please use the space below for this purpose.

See the end of this chapter for our comments (p. 92).

*Exercise 5.13: Asking the right questions*

Please comment on the wording of the following questions taken from a range of questionnaires. **How well are the questions phrased?** Think about the responses you might get from the questions asked.

**Your comment**

| 1  How satisfactory was your stay at the Carlton Hotel? | |
|---|---|

| 2 What is your place of residence? | |
|---|---|
| 3 Some people say that the city is spending too much on building new schools. Do you agree or disagree? | |
| 4 How much time did you spend reading the newspaper yesterday? | |
| 5 What is your religion? | |

| 6 How old are you? | |
|---|---|
| 7 Does your employer make adequate provision for maternity/paternity leave? | |

See the end of this chapter for our comments (p. 93).

*How to prevent your questionnaire from being binned*

There are techniques and tips that can help improve response rates to postal or electronic questionnaires:

- **Most important, check for spelling mistakes and grammatical errors**: correct every error, otherwise your questionnaire may end up in the rubbish bin.
- **Make contact with the research subjects in advance**: tell them about the aim and purpose of the research. You can establish, from the response of the person, whether or not it is worth sending the questionnaire.
- **Always include a covering letter**: explain the purpose of the questionnaire and enclose a stamped return envelope for postal questionnaires.
- **Personalize the questionnaire**: if possible, write to the person by name.
- **Emphasize confidentiality**: explain that all views to be published will remain anonymous, unless permission is given for names to be used.
- **Share findings**: offer to share the research findings with any participant.
- **Give contact details**: include contact details and offer to discuss the aim and purpose of the questionnaire with any recipient who has doubts or queries about it.
- **Make follow-up calls**: use telephone reminders or special delivery reminder letters to encourage people to respond.

### Group discussions or focus groups

Group discussions or focus groups can be an effective way to gather data from a selected group of people. The process can be a useful way of finding out what the main issues and concerns of any group are. This can help in the questionnaire design stage or to develop a future interview strategy.

They can also bring to the surface issues that might not otherwise have been discovered; for example, people can often be bolder in advancing their opinions in groups, particularly when others agree with them.

The researcher should create a relaxed atmosphere and record in some way what is being said (for example, by use of a tape-recorder, video camera or neutral note-taker).

The purpose of the discussion should be introduced and discussion ground-rules agreed. The researcher encourages free discussion and plays a neutral role, but is ready to intervene to resolve any problems that occur.

*Exercise 5.14:  Under what circumstances might the researcher intervene during a group discussion? Write in the space below.*

See the end of this chapter for our comments (p. 94).

### Methodology checklist

Imagine your tutor was asking you the following questions – can you answer them? Tick either 'Yes' or 'No'. (Ignore any questions not relevant to your research.)

| Question | Yes | No |
|---|---|---|
| 1 Have you decided which **approach** to adopt for your research, for example, qualitative/quantitative or inductive/deductive? | | |
| 2 Can you explain why you will adopt this approach? | | |
| 3 Have you decided which **methods** (tools) you will use to gather primary and/or secondary data? | | |
| 4 Can you say why you decided on these particular methods? | | |
| 5 Have you decided what criteria you will adopt for collecting data (for example, target number, age, gender, occupation)? | | |
| 6 Have you decided upon a target sample number for data collection? | | |
| 7 Can you explain the type of sample it will be? | | |
| 8 Do you know where and how you will collect data? | | |
| 9 Have you anticipated what logistical or other problems you might encounter in collecting or analysing the data? | | |
| 10 Have you worked out how you will record the data? | | |
| 11 Have you worked out how you will collate the data? | | |
| 12 Have you worked out how you will analyse the collated data? | | |

### Stages of research

The main stages of research are summarized in a personal research activity. However, the transition between one stage and another is not always so clear-cut. For example, it may be necessary to go back and forth between stages to collect additional data, to do further reading, or to adjust a timetable. Nevertheless, you should plan a timetable and identify target dates for the completion of each stage, as suggested in the personal research activity log.

### Personal research activity: planning target dates for your research

For each of the main stages of research, fill in your target date.

| | |
|---|---|
| 1 Establish a general field of interest; discuss with supervisor/tutor. | **Your target date for this stage:** |
| 2 Undertake preliminary and background reading on the subject to be researched, to discover what is known already and to suggest the choice of an appropriate research methodology. | **Your target date for this stage:** |
| 3 Narrow your ideas to a workable topic or research proposal and give it a title. Decide on the most appropriate methods for gathering data; discuss this with your tutor, if applicable. | **Your target date for this stage:** |
| 4 Prepare information gathering 'tools', for example, questionnaires, interview sheets. | **Your target date for this stage:** |
| 5 Gather information. This can take a significant amount of work, so allow plenty of time for this. | **Your target date for this stage:** |
| 6 Collate, analyse and interpret research data. This can take a significant amount of time, so plan accordingly. | **Your target date for this stage:** |
| 7 Write first draft of research project report; discuss with your tutor, if applicable. | **Your target date for this stage:** |
| 8 Revise and rewrite dissertation; submit dissertation project. | **Your target date for this stage:** |

### Common research problems

The most common research problems you may encounter include the following.

- Underestimating the amount of work to final completion.
- Being over-optimistic about the number of completed questionnaires returned to you.
- Coping with a long piece of work.
- Lacking organization, particularly failing to keep notes and record references.
- Failing to take a critical or analytical perspective.
- Suffering from a lack of focus.
- Relying only on supervisors.

#### Underestimating the amount of work to final completion

This can be a problem, particularly at the data collection and collation stages, and in the final writing stages. Remember, you are unlikely to be able to write your report in just one draft. It is likely to need revision before you and your tutor are satisfied with it.

#### Being over-optimistic about the number of completed questionnaires that will be returned to you

Be realistic about the target you set for yourself. Give people a good reason to fill in your questionnaire or to talk to you and allow them enough time to do it. If you achieve a 25–30 per cent return for a postal questionnaire, you will have done well.

#### Coping with a long piece of work

Research can be a very tiring process, particularly in the latter stages. Build rest days into your time schedule; don't work every day of the week on your research.

#### Lacking organization, particularly failing to keep notes and record references

A lack of organization, particularly about organizing your notes, will catch you out. For example, it can be infuriating if you want to cite a source in your report, but then realize you have lost details of the source – or failed to note the details properly in the first place.

#### Failing to take a critical or analytical perspective

This problem concerns being overly descriptive when you should be analytical, or reaching conclusions without much supporting evidence, or even as a result of guesswork.

### Suffering from a lack of focus

This can happen when no clear points or conclusions emerge from the research. To avoid this situation, you need to be clear from the start what specific questions you want to address in the project – and keep focused on these.

### Relying only on supervisors

Your supervisor is an important source of help, but you must not rely exclusively on him or her for total support! You can get help from other students, the Learner Support Unit at your institution, friends, and relatives. It is a good idea to talk about your research to as many people who will listen to you; explaining it to someone else helps you clarify your goals.

## Comments on and answers to the exercises in this chapter

This section provides comments on and answers to the exercises you may have attempted earlier in this chapter.

---

### Exercise 5.1: Finding sources

- Ask your supervisor or other tutors for suggestions.
- Look at the bibliographies of peer-reviewed journal articles written on the topic for other relevant sources.
- Talk to the subject librarians – they have a very good all-round knowledge and can direct you to relevant sources in both printed and electronic forms.
- Search for unpublished dissertations written by other students on a similar or related topic, and look at the sources in their bibliographies.
- Ask experts inside or outside the university. For example, don't be afraid to send an email to an academic who has written on the research topic. You can ask them to advise you on who is currently researching in the topic area, so you can contact them to both share and gain knowledge.

---

### Exercise 5.2: Identifying primary and secondary sources

**Primary sources can include:**

- Articles in peer-reviewed academic journals (printed or online).
- Books written by the originator of a particular theory, idea, model or practice.
- Critics of the ideas expressed in journals, books or media, providing they have built a strong reputation for intelligent comment in the subject area.
- Originators of creative work, e.g. authors, artists, musicians, film and stage directors.
- Conference papers presenting original research or ideas by their originators.

- Reports written by the originators of proposals, particularly if supported by an influential body, agency or institution.
- Original court and parliamentary proceedings.
- Autobiographies.
- Minutes of important meetings.

**Secondary sources can include:**

- Professional or trade journals, unless they were presenting original research findings.
- Newspaper reports.
- Tutor handouts (unless presenting original work by the tutor).
- Text books summarizing the work of others.
- Reference books.
- Wiki Internet sites.
- Other Internet sites summarizing the work of others.
- Biographies.
- Student dissertations.
- Unpublished conference papers.

---

*Exercise 5.3: What questions could you ask to determine the credibility of a source?*

*General questions*

- Is the publisher or originator of the evidence a reputable one?
- Are sources of evidence presented done so in a credible way, e.g. properly referenced?
- Does the bibliography presented by the author seem comprehensive and wide in its coverage?
- Does the author present all relevant background and context information of the ideas presented, e.g. explain in a convincing way the rationale to his or her ideas?
- Is the information presented still valid? For example, if it was written over five years ago, are the ideas still applicable today?
- If it is a research finding, is the research methodology carefully presented to the reader?

*Questions specifically about electronic sources*

- Do your tutors recommend this Internet site?
- Why has this site been established – is it clear from the introduction?
- Who sponsors and/or pays for the site?
- Who is the intended readership for the site?
- Are there any open or possible biases in the site?
- Were you linked to this site from a reliable source?
- Does it **look** professional?
- Is the site easy to navigate and use?
- Does the resource follow good principles of design, proper grammar, spelling and style?
- Was the site updated recently?

*Exercise 5.4: Ethical case study on store assistants*

You would have two main choices in this situation. The first involves concealing your research role identity from the other members of staff at the store. The second involves requesting permission from the store management and revealing your research aim and purposes to all the staff involved. Both options raise ethical concerns for you as researcher; as follows:

*Concealment of research identity*

This option raises significant questions of ethics, as you would be, in effect, 'spying' on colleagues for your own purposes. They might also have shared information with you in confidence; information they would not expect you to divulge to others. You could argue, however, that what you learned and reported could be to the longer-term advantage of staff morale and overall efficiency of the store. But, the store managers might argue – particularly if your research findings were critical of them – that your findings were subjective and biased, because of your own employee position in the store and because you did not canvas opinions from others involved.

*Declaration of research identity*

This option also raises important ethical issues to consider, including:

- How will you approach gaining permission for this project? Will all the staff be involved and consulted? If not, why not?
- How will the staff **feel** about being observed by you? Might they feel threatened and worried? What would you say to reassure them?
- How might staff members **respond** to being observed by you? In what ways might their attitudes and behaviour change towards you?
- What records would you keep? When and how would you make notes – at the time, or afterwards? If afterwards, how long afterwards?
- How possible is it for you to act as a store assistant **and** a participant observer of events in the store? Would there be a role conflict in any way? If so, how?
- Would you use the real names of staff members? Or would you keep their identities anonymous? If their identities were kept anonymous, would it still be possible to identify individuals from their quoted words or reported deeds?
- Will individual staff members have an opportunity to read what you have recorded and commented about them? What would you do if they objected to what you had written about them?
- Who will see your findings? Will all the staff involved be able to see and comment on your findings? If not, why not?
- What might be the outcome of your research be for certain members of staff you felt were the most culpable or responsible? Might they lose their jobs?

*Exercise 5.5: Seven ethical issues for researches*

1   Issues concerning the rights of privacy of individuals.
2   Issues concerning the voluntary nature of participation – and the rights of individuals to withdraw partially or completely from the process.
3   Issues around confidentiality and the maintenance of the confidentiality of data provided by participants.
4   Issues around obtaining the consent and possible deception of participants (see Exercise 5.4).
5   Issues around responding to the reactions of participants to the ways in which researchers seek to collect data.
6   Issues around the effects on participants of the way in which data are analysed and reported.
7   Issues around the behaviour and objectivity of the researcher.

*Exercise 5.6: What do you think are the main advantages/positives and disadvantages/negatives of both positivistic and phenomenological approaches in research?*

### Positivistic

| Advantages/Positives | Disadvantages/Negatives |
| --- | --- |
| • Suitable for research projects that require a structured and qualitative approach.<br>• Can be effective for research projects that are, for example, descriptive in nature; e.g. to identify and quantify the element parts of any phenomenon.<br>• Standardization of approach to research can make collation and codifying of gathered data easier.<br>• Research methods easier to reproduce and, therefore, easier for other researchers to test your conclusions. | • Highly structured research design imposes prearranged limits and boundaries to research.<br>• Limited approach to take if you are trying to explain **why** things happen.<br>• Assumes that researchers can be totally objective; but researchers may allow their own values to influence the approach, for example in the questions posed.<br>• It is very difficult to capture the complex interplay of phenomena in a single measure.<br>• You need a large sample to be able to make generalizations from results. |

### Phenomenological

| Advantages/Postives | Disadvantages/Negatives |
| --- | --- |
| • Lets you use a relatively small sample for your studies.<br>• Enables you to gather data that are 'rich' in personal comment and personal insights.<br>• Enables you to explore below the presenting surface of an issue. | • The findings are subjective; it can be difficult to assert wider, more generalized points from the research.<br>• Your findings and conclusions are vulnerable to the charge that they cannot be substantiated.<br>• Your research may be hard for other researchers to test. |

*Exercise 5.7: What sampling strategy was used in this study?*

In the early 1990s a study examined the personal characteristics of 50 highly successful independent retailers. The 50 were contacted through business networks across England. The names of potential respondents were passed to the researchers by the chairs of these networks. The researchers wrote to the retailers concerned and invited them to participate in the survey, which included the completion of a questionnaire and interview with the researcher.

**Answer: This was an example of purposive sampling (non-probability).**

*Exercise 5.8: What types of research project might favour a structured interview approach?*

Research projects that aim to be **descriptive in nature**, or where you are aiming for high reliability (the research findings can be tested more easily by other researchers using same methodology). This approach to interview is suitable for gathering data that can then be analysed in a precise way.

*Exercise 5.9: What types of research project might favour a semi-structured or unstructured interview approach?*

Semi-structured or unstructured interview approaches can be suitable for research projects that are **exploratory** or **explanatory** in nature: to discover and account for the 'why' (reasons/motives) for things that happen. They can also be suitable for research that seeks to understand and explain the relationships between variables, or where you need to seek for new insights into a subject.

*Exercise 5.10: How might bias affect the responses of the interviewer and interviewee?*

A range of factors, based on stereotypes, can affect our perceptions, including gender, race, age, speech, appearance and attitude. We may be, for example, favourably or unfavourably disposed towards younger or older people; we might be racially biased; or our perceptions may be coloured by particular accents, or by the clothes that people wear. Sexual bias is a particularly significant factor. Rosenthal (1966), for example, suggested that both male and female researchers behave more warmly towards female subjects than they do towards male subjects. There is a perception, perhaps, that female subjects are more tolerant of being interviewed; whereas men may be more unpredictable in their responses and attitudes if stopped by an interviewer.

**Exercise 5.11: What do you think are the respective research advantages and disadvantages of asking open and closed questions?**

## Open questions

| Advantages | Disadvantages |
|---|---|
| • Enables you to get below the surface to explore and probe issues.<br>• Allows respondents to offer more considered answers.<br>• Encourages respondents to give honest opinions. | • The responses can be hard to collate.<br>• The research may be difficult for others to reproduce, so your findings are open to doubt or question. |

## Closed questions

| Advantages | Disadvantages |
|---|---|
| • Often easier for respondents (particularly those who are busy) to answer.<br>• Easier to collate than open questions.<br>• The questionnaire can be easily reproduced by other researchers. | • They limit the choices of answers to respondents.<br>• It is harder for the researcher to get below the surface of an issue if only limited or superficial answers are presented. |

**Exercise 5.12: Scaling the responses to questions**

'How would you describe your parents' attitude to higher education at the time you applied?' It is unclear whether the question is aimed at students of all ages, or only those still within the jurisdiction of their parents. There is also an assumption that there is more than one 'parent' on the scene – and that they are both alive. The student receiving the questionnaire may be older, i.e. a mature student, and independent of his or her parents. In the case of a younger student, his or her parents may both be dead; or there may be only one parent; or the respondent may be in the care or guardianship of others. And what about the situation where two parents have differing views? The question should, therefore, be rephrased to take into account a range of family situations and differing views.

### Exercise 5.13: *Asking the right questions*

| | | **Our comment** |
|---|---|---|
| 1 | How satisfactory was your stay at the Carlton Hotel? | This is a vague question and it would be better to ask questions relating to **specific aspects** of the person's stay in the hotel, e.g. cleanliness of the rooms, courtesy of staff, choice of meals. |
| 2 | What is your place of residence? | This question is open to misinterpretation, as 'place of residence' might be regarded as a road, town, county or country. |
| 3 | Some people say that the city is spending too much on building new schools. Do you agree or disagree? | This question presents just one perspective on the topic. It would be better to include both perspectives; for example, 'Some people say that the city is spending too much on building new schools, while others argue not enough is being spent? What is your view?' |
| 4 | How much time did you spend reading the newspaper yesterday? | There is an assumption being made that the person did or should have read a newspaper. Respondents faced with such a question may be tempted to make something up to save face. |
| 5 | What is your religion? | This question assumes the respondent has an affiliation to a particular religion. It is better to offer respondents a choice of religious groups, as well as options for atheists, agnostics and others. |
| 6 | How old are you? | This is a stark and abrupt way of asking a sensitive question, and some respondents might take offence at it. It is better to offer respondents a choice of boxes to tick with age cohorts, for example 30–39, 40–49, 50–59, or ask for a year of birth. |
| 7 | Does your employer make adequate provision for maternity/paternity leave? | The word 'adequate' is vague and imprecise and may be based on a model of maternity/paternity leave arrangement known to the researcher, but not to the participant. It would be better to simply ask what provision the respondent's employer makes for maternity/paternity leave. |

**Research Skills and Orientations**  First steps to good research

*Exercise 5.14:  Under what circumstances might the researcher intervene during a group discussion?*

The researcher may need to consider intervening in the following kinds of situations:
- If one group member is dominating the discussion.
- If the group strayed from discussing the topic in question.
- To encourage quieter members of the group to contribute to the discussion.
- To resolve any conflicts that arose between group members.

## Chapter summary: Key learning points

- Recognize that research is not a single activity or something that you do later in your studies: it is a fundamental part of being a student and it pays to know about research and adopt a research orientation as early as possible during your studies.
- Explore the many different ways of carrying out research: all of these methods have accompanying strengths and weaknesses.
- Be aware that engaging in research can help you to use and understand evidence and will be useful in helping you to develop and sharpen your critical thinking skills.
- Understand that research involves conjecture, search, creativity, analysis and discovery – it can be an exciting and creative part of your life as a student.

### Suggested further reading

Bell, J. (2005) *Doing your Research Project*, 4th edn. Maidenhead: Open University Press.
Blaxter, L., Hughes, C. and Tight, M. (2006) *How to Research*, 3rd edn. Maidenhead: Open University Press.
Denscombe, M. (2007) *The Good Research Guide for Small-Scale Research Projects*, 3rd edn. Maidenhead: Open University Press.
Oliver, P. (1997) *Research*. London: Teach Yourself.
Wallimann, N. (2004) *Your Undergraduate Dissertation: The Essential Guide for Success*. London: Sage.

# Getting It On Paper: Learning the skills for confident academic writing

**6**

## Chapter Contents

## Chapter Overview

- **Getting to grips with academic writing**
- **Recognizing that writing can sometimes be stressful**
- **Developing useful techniques for developing your writing fluency**
- **Understanding the benefits of good outlines**
- **Recognizing the common features of academic writing**
- **Getting writing advice from an expert**

## Introduction

The blank page has the power to crush even some of the most confident and self-possessed of students. It is going to be an enormous help if you are able to write well and productively at college in ways that give rise to good grades and other good outcomes for you.

Academic writing is not an uncomplicated task. It involves a wide range of different kinds of skills and if you are going to do it properly, it means that you have to know clearly what is required of you and how to deliver it. The skill of writing at university is not a simple or straightforward one and it demands a range of interconnected capacities that you may not feel you have yet mastered. But writing essays, reports, literature reviews and other assignments can be much more interesting and satisfying than you might first expect.

This chapter aims to help you to tap into the inherently creative and even occasionally exciting process that writing at college can represent for you. So instead of seeing the blank page as a curse, you might be more likely to see it as an inviting canvas, waiting for you to make your mark with confidence and with style.

We would like to reassure you that even though academic writing can feel difficult, boring, stressful and daunting, there are other possibilities buried under the surface of every writing task. This is particularly true if you can confront any worries and fears you have about academic writing.

If you circled the more negative emotions and experiences (frustration, uncertainty, fear, stress, anxiety, boredom or irritation) you are not alone. Many students talk about these kinds of feelings when they think about their academic writing tasks and the demands associated with them. If you circled the more positive emotions (curiosity, excitement, delight, joy, determination, motivation or confidence), then you are in the lucky position of having a lot of positive energy to work with in pursuit of your writing goals. For many people, writing-related emotions are a mix of positive and negative, and that too is to be expected. But even if the associations you have are all negative, it is still possible to do a few things that will increase the likelihood that you will come to enjoy and be more confident and positive about the writing process.


## Getting to grips with academic writing

As you face any academic writing task, it is worth asking yourself a range of important questions. Learning to answer them can then become your strategy for making writing a positive, pleasurable part of your life as a student. The main reasons that people grapple with academic writing and find it difficult and stressful are generally due to the following kinds of issues:

- Not feeling as if academic writing can be creative or enjoyable.
- Not knowing enough about the 'rules' of academic writing.
- Not feeling confident enough about the things you have been asked to write about.
- Not planning out the writing task in advance.
- Not managing time and leaving too much to the last minute.
- Not being prepared to revise.

(Adapted from Moore 2008)

---

***Exercise 6.1: Your orientation towards academic writing – a reflective quiz***

Take a few minutes to think about your own feelings towards academic writing. You might like to think about the last essay you were asked to write, or a writing task that you know you're going to have to complete in the near future. How does or did this writing task make you feel? What kinds of emotions can you describe that are associated with this task? Circle any of the ones below that seem most relevant to you:

Frustration

Uncertainty

Curiosity

Excitement

Fear

Stress

Anxiety

Delight

Joy

Determination

Motivation

Boredom

Irritation

Confidence

---

### Focusing on enjoyment

Many students have told us that they did not always hate writing as much as they sometimes discover they do when faced with writing tasks at university. Many talk about the joy they used to derive from writing creative essays at school or writing stories or emailing their friends with long explanations of what they think or how they feel. Something seems to happen when a student's first academic writing deadline looms at college: suddenly the structured, very stylized requirements they encounter when facing writing tasks makes writing feel like a very different prospect. Many students tell us that it is because they feel there are so many 'rules' associated with academic writing that make them feel it is a tortured, difficult thing to do. There is a sense of the 'reader over the shoulder' waiting always for them to make a false move. Their anxiety about writing things well, accurately and correctly, makes the mountain feel very difficult to climb.

It is true: there are many rules associated with academic writing. It is possibly because of those rules that students often feel there is no room left for their own ideas, their own opinions, their own voices. And feeling voiceless is probably the worst condition to be in when you're preparing to write an essay.

### Forgetting the rules – at least at the beginning of the process

In order to make writing feel motivating, interesting and creative, we recommend that at least for the first draft of any written piece, you temporarily forget about the rules and regulations associated with academic writing (apart that is from the rule of not copying other people's writing and passing it off as your own – see Chapter 7 for a more detailed discussion on the pitfalls of plagiarism). That is not to say that the rules should be ignored completely or forever. It is just that if you are too worried about the rules, you can forget to generate your own ideas or to be clearer about what you think the different aspects of a particular writing task should contain. This is the key to ensuring that your own voice has a chance of positioning itself among the voices of other experts and writers that will subsequently serve to inform and contextualize what you have written.

---

### Exercise 6.2: Freewriting

Pick a writing assignment that you have been given to complete. Instead of starting with reading sources and literature from elsewhere, free yourself to write about it in an unstructured, rule-free, fluid kind of a way. Create a prompt for yourself such as: what do I know about this topic or what questions might I need to ask to find out more about it, or what interesting angles might be useful to consider about it? Write your prompt at the top of the page and then write freely, messily, chaotically even, about the ideas that develop. Here are some of the things that might help you to keep writing during this freewriting exercise:

- Write for a specific amount of time and try to keep writing even if you feel your ideas are clunky or uninformed or incomplete. For your first freewriting exercise, select a pretty short timeframe. Ten minutes is a good timeframe to start with. Stick to that timeframe and give yourself the freedom to let yourself see what comes out of your head and onto the page during that time.
- Try to write in full sentences – not single words or lists or shorthand. Try to give your ideas as much room to be fully articulated as you can.
- Do not be tempted to edit or correct or cross things out as you write. This is not an exercise in perfection, but an exercise in 'exuberant imperfection' (Baty 2004), giving you room to play with ideas, to tap into your own notions and concepts and to build your writing from there.
- Be prepared to be surprised by the ideas you come up with, but also do not expect it to happen too quickly. You might need to practise this activity a few times before your ideas start to flow.

### Knowing the rules

In our experience, it is a really good thing to start with your own questions, ideas, orientations and instincts by engaging in freewriting exercises like the one we outlined in the previous section. But if your academic writing is going to transform itself into something that will get a good grade, you need to know how to take a messy, unstructured piece of writing and transform it into something that observes the rules and requirements of academia. So it is important to know the rules that are generally associated with academic writing so that you can make sure you give yourself every chance to present your writing in a way that will allow you to get good grades, but that also you learn and absorb information that helps you to get on top of your discipline. You need to strike a balance between being influenced by the expert voices and ideas of other people and also giving your own voice room to be seen and heard within any piece of written work.

### What makes writing academic?

There are some general rules associated with academic writing. These rules typically require you to be clear and explicit about what you are writing, to be objective and detached about the arguments you make and the conclusions that you draw, to refer to and discuss the perspectives of well-known writers and experts on the topic you are writing about, to use evidence to support or question particular perspectives and ideas and to adopt a 'critical stance' towards the arguments and concepts that you are exploring. Table 6.1 outlines in more detail what each of those characteristics means.

### Developing a college-based writing strategy and managing time

It is not true to say that the more time you have, the better your writing will be. Sometimes a stiff deadline is a great way of helping you to focus your mind and get down to it. But however much or little time you have to complete a writing assignment, managing that time is still a very important part of your strategy. There are good tips for general time management in Chapter 8 which are useful for managing your schedule and balancing everything you need to do.

Particularly for writing tasks keep in mind the following time management principles. First, **regular, small bouts of writing can help to keep your work on track** (Murray and Moore 2006). While you may need to take a couple of all nighters to reach a tight deadline and while we know that this is not always avoidable, we still recommend that instead of trying to pull together a lot of writing only at the times when you are under pressure to produce it, you should plan to write regularly for small stretches of time – say half an hour to an hour every day.

Second, getting into the writing habit and **doing it regularly** can help to make you more fluent and confident about all your writing tasks. If, for example, you have a definite time for writing every day and if you build that time slot firmly into your schedule, then you provide yourself

| Table 6.1 Features of academic text (characteristics of academic writing that are commonly valued and expected) | |
|---|---|
| Explication | Academic texts lay out in explicit terms the aims and scope of their content. They tend to provide a roadmap of key hypotheses, arguments and ideas, and they usually contain conclusions that reiterate and re-emphasize these key dimensions of the text |
| Objectivity/detachment | Academic texts typically establish a detached and objective orientation to the topics they explore. There tends to be a 'rhetorical distance' between the reader and the writer |
| Intertextuality: references to other texts | Academic texts are possibly most distinguished from other forms of text by frequent reference to the ideas, research or perspectives of other writers in the field. These references are cited in highly conventional and rule-bound ways |
| Rationality | Academic texts often display a rational, logical and 'scientific' approach to argument, evidence and 'proof'. This scientific approach has come to dominate many fields of academic inquiry, even where such an approach may not be strictly necessary or even appropriate |
| Critical thinking | Academic writing tends to be more valued if it demonstrates a critical approach to the material it is exploring. A critical approach requires not taking evidence or explanations at face value, finding ways of exploring and exposing underlying assumptions and challenging prevailing dogma or 'received wisdom' |

(Adapted from Borg 2008)

with a regular, focused and reliable forum in which to sharpen all the skills associated with writing. Third, if you have sketched out a good outline and tackle a small part of that outline each day, you may be amazed to discover how quickly a particular writing assignment comes together (Murray 2006).

## Responding to feedback

In the earlier stages of writing, you should not worry too much about your audience. When gathering ideas by using techniques like freewriting, or when generating your very first messy draft, you might be horrified by the thought of showing your writing to anyone else. But as your work takes shape, feedback from other people can help you to make sure that what you are producing makes sense, is clear, comes across the way you want it to and does not miss important ideas or arguments (Elbow and Belanoff 2000). It is really useful to show your work to somebody else before you submit it. Some universities have writing centres or writing clinics that provide this service to students; even if yours does not, finding someone who will read your work before you submit it may help you to polish and develop it in a way that will make it much better – sometimes small changes and improvements based on other people's reading of your work, can make a big difference to the quality of your final written submission.

### There is no such thing as good writing – just good rewriting

The redrafting process should be an essential part of your writing strategy. Many students adopt the approach that their writing can be produced in a single draft. For the vast majority of people, this is a big mistake. As soon as you get used to the redrafting process, your writing will improve in all sorts of important ways. Your first draft is never going to present all the work you have put in, in its best light. Many experienced writers produce as many as a dozen drafts of their work, each one becoming successively better, sharper, clearer and more coherent. That may seem like an awful lot of redrafting for your purposes, but we recommend that you commit to producing up to four drafts of your written assignment before you finalize and submit it.

This is how your four drafts might be broadly described.

- **Draft 1: The rough draft**
  Rough, messy, full of ideas, working to your original outline.

- **Draft 2: The working document**
  Tidier, more coherent, cleaner, more precise with whole new sections inserted, and at least some of the material from draft 1 deleted, improved or amended.

- **Draft 3: The penultimate draft**
  Incorporating feedback from another reader, changes benefiting from the views of another person, crisper and cleaner and well referenced according to citation conventions.

- **Draft 4: The final proof**
  Picking up any final typos, edits and minor errors to make sure the piece is word perfect.

### The writing process: from prewriting to letting it go

As you progress through your writing task, it is useful to be aware that there are different stages of the process (e.g. Hjortshoj 2001) that can be named, and it is useful for you to know roughly where you are in that process. The five stages comprise prewriting, composing, revising, editing and letting it go.

#### *Prewriting*

This includes anything that is going to help you to get down to the job of writing. It could involve keeping a list of ideas in a notebook, finding and reading about other sources of information, research or evidence, talking and listening to other people about the focus of your writing etc. Be careful though that prewriting really does eventually lead you to sit down and start writing. Sometimes people sabotage their writing goals by spending too much time getting ready to write, and not enough (if any) time actually sitting down to do it.

## Composing

This is the phase of writing that has you sitting down and tapping away furiously at the keyboard. Particularly for the first draft, getting ideas on paper or on screen, elaborating and developing them, bringing your ideas to light by writing them down, should be as fluent and unfettered a process as you can possibly make it. At the first composition phase you should give yourself permission to be messy, open ended and loosely structured, even if you are writing to an outline and even if you are finding that outline helpful in directing and containing your ideas and arguments.

## Revising

This is the redrafting phase and you may find as we have mentioned, that you need to redraft several times before you are happy that you have produced something in writing that is as good as it can be. The revision process allows you to cast a colder, more objective eye on your work, to sharpen what is good and to discard what is not useful in the text that you have produced.

## Editing

Editing is really the final revision, the process you engage in just before you submit your written work. This is the phase where you are making sure that the grammar and spelling are all correct and that you have used consistent heading and subheading styles, observed the citation conventions, included a cover page, inserted page numbers and that everything in general looks neat, well presented and in order.

## Letting it go

You can fall into a trap, if you are not aware of it, of endlessly trying to finish or perfect a piece of writing. There does come a time when you have to let it go – otherwise you risk undermining it or messing with parts of it that are already pretty good. If you stay with the task and engage with the redrafting process, you should reach a stage where it is as ready as it can be. Be prepared to let it go when you feel it is good enough.

## Nourishing your writing with the ideas and perspectives of others

Most people who get used to freewriting find that quite quickly they can produce a bunch of messy interesting ideas, questions and possible directions for their writing, no matter what the writing task happens to be. So try practising and see what happens for you and your ideas. In addition, if you review Table 6.1 a few times, you will have a clearer idea about the features that you have to ensure are part of your written piece. As well as this though, in order to produce a good piece of academic writing you will need to do some reading too. You can get some helpful ideas about how to research information about an academic topic in Chapter 5 and there are some useful tips about reading and taking in information in Chapter 4.

---

When starting to write about any topic, here are some of the questions you should ask when searching for and integrating other sources into your own writing:

1   Who has written about this topic before? Can you find a list of well-quoted writers, researchers and commentators who are commonly known to have worked on this topic?
2   From what you read and how you reflect on the topic, can you identify what the 'current state of knowledge' is? In other words, are there current views and assumptions that seem to be widely held by the experts whose work you have read?
3   What are the different definitions, concepts and issues relevant to this topic?
4   How has thinking about this topic changed over the years?
5   What are the different theories associated with this topic?
6   What are the key points of disagreement in the existing literature?
7   Are there unanswered questions or untackled problems associated with the topic and what does the literature say about any attempts that have been made to tackle them?
8   What are the main directions for future research that have been recommended by writers and researchers in the field?

(Adapted from Moore and Murphy 2005)

---

These questions will allow you to engage in reading that can inform your writing and will enable you to sharpen your ideas and questions so that your writing will be more scholarly and well contextualized. Such questions can be used for any of the writing tasks you engage in, and will also have the added benefit of really helping you to get on top of a subject quite quickly.

### Imposing structure on your writing: the benefits of a good outline

Another useful tool in your academic writing tool kit is the ability to sketch a good outline for your written piece. It is enormously helpful to have an outline; it gives you a good route map and helps to develop coherence and structure in your writing. It helps you to build your arguments in ways that make sense both to you as a writer and to your readers and it helps to ensure that the final written output will be tight and strong, avoiding common pitfalls such as unnecessary repetition or loose ends.

Creating a good outline simply involves generating headings and subheadings that create a scaffolding around your writing task. Usually your lecturers/tutors will specify a word count – if they do not, you should ask them to – and this is a useful measure for you to judge how much writing you need to devote to each section of your written piece. Organize your writing into identifiable parts – for example in the case of an essay you might include main sections such as an introduction, a review of literature, a series of propositions, a focus on key aspects of the debate/idea/issue, a discussion of evidence, and then a concluding section. Each of these sections will contain a number of ideas which you should name and lay out as a sort of 'writing map'. Below is a sample outline for an essay. You can adapt the process for any topic or for any academic writing task. Remember, that some assignments will specify very clear sections and outlines that are required for different parts of your writing, while others will be looser and more ambiguous. In the latter case, it will help if you impose the structure of an outline on the task yourself.

### *Sample economics essay outline*

Essay topic: Many economic commentators say that, because of recent economic events, capitalism is dead. Discuss.

Introduction (500 words)

- What this essay is about and what it will argue.
- Definition of capitalism.
- Brief identification of relevant recent events that have undermined the notion of capitalism.

Literature review (1000 words)

- Writers who have historically supported the notion of capitalism.
- Writers who have opposed the notion of capitalism.
- Problems, issues, strengths and weaknesses of a capitalist system.

Recent events (1500 words)

- Tracing the origins and development of global recession.
- Key global events that have undermined capitalism and why.
- Implications for the future of the world economy.

Conclusions (1000 words)

- Is capitalism dead? Your conclusions based on the ideas and events discussed above.
- Further unresolved questions and issues for the future.
- Quick summary.

This gives you a sample of an outline for a particular kind of essay on a very specific topic. You can quickly generate your own outlines of this kind, no matter what the topic you have been asked to write about.

### Staying flexible and avoiding the tyranny of outlines

While outlines can help you to structure and sequence your writing, do not let your outline impose excessive restrictions on the discoveries that you might uncover on the way. It is good to be structured when you are producing academic writing, but it is also important – vital even – to stay flexible. Writing is not only the transmission of ideas from your head to the page, but also a hugely generative process in its own right. The real beauty of writing is not its ability to show what you already know – the magic of writing lies in its ability to generate new ideas as you write. The very act of writing can help new ideas to spring into your mind, producing words on paper or on screen can spark new directions, new questions and new insights that will be marvellous new fuel for your unique contribution. As well as a structure, you need to give yourself permission to allow your writing to take you in new directions, directions that you might not have been able to predict or identify at the beginning of a writing task. So at the very least, you may need to change your outline several times before you reach the end of your writing task. Give yourself enough room (and time) to allow new ideas, sections or issues to occur to you as you become more confident and knowledgeable about your topic and give yourself the permission to take your writing to unknown places. By doing this, you will be more likely to strike a balance between the important need to structure your writing and the important process of developing, enhancing and enriching the knowledge and insights that your writing can bring to the subjects you are learning about.

### Some advice from a writing expert

The following notes are **from Peter Elbow** (to see Peter's full discussion on the topic of writing, check out **www.youtube.com/watch?v=mrcq3dzt0Uk**)

### *Our primary and strongest relationship with language is through speaking*

We do not have to think about grammatical complexity; spoken language is linked with the body, it's not just cognitive. It can be very useful to exploit your natural, fluent ability to speak, when you are trying to develop your writing. So, If you are finding it difficult to write, try talking it out – say your ideas out loud. Recruit the help of a peer or someone who has a similar task and have a brainstorm that will allow you to. Your own natural language skills will help you to articulate and clarify some of the things that you can then start writing about. Use freewriting to write something in a natural, conversational kind of way, and then at least you have raw material to work with. After that you can go back and develop, craft, clarify and nuance what you want your final draft to look like. That you speak more freely and fluently than you are likely to be able to write is natural – try applying this natural skill to the development of your writing competencies.

### *The same words cause different things to happen in different minds*

You are never going to be able to write the perfect piece. Keep in mind that anything you write is going to be interpreted differently by different people. Do not get too paralysed by the

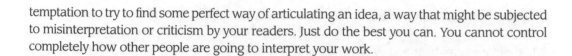

temptation to try to find some perfect way of articulating an idea, a way that might be subjected to misinterpretation or criticism by your readers. Just do the best you can. You cannot control completely how other people are going to interpret your work.

### It is impossible to give a valid, reliable single number grade to a piece of writing – because there are many dimensions to writing

Even if your writing has to be submitted and graded, keep in mind that experts in writing now say that it is impossible to give a single grade to any piece of academic writing. There are so many different features of writing (structure, clarity, creativity, validity, imagination, expression, style, precision etc.) – the grade you receive may reflect only some of these criteria, and completely ignore other aspects of your writing that may be strong. It is very important to try to find out from the people who are assessing your writing, what are the criteria that they are going to assess you on. Table 6.1 above outlines the features of academic writing, but do not assume that all tutors/lecturers grade with these features in mind. Make sure you know the kinds of things that your assessors are looking for. Learn to adapt your writing to achieve different kinds of criteria for different assignments or writing contexts.

### It pays to take yourself seriously as a writer

When people feel like they are writers, when 'writer' is part of their identity, they are more likely to invest time and energy and optimism into their writing tasks. Instead of seeing yourself as a student who has to do a lot of writing, try developing a sense that part of what you are is a writer. Developing your identity as a writer helps learners to feel like they want to write and internalize their writing habits, and become more regular writers.

### Many people hate and fear writing but many people love writing and when they do they seem to love it a lot and keep wanting to do it

People feel strongly about writing. People express strong feelings about their writing activities. Writing is an emotionally charged experience invoking stress, anxiety, fear, excitement, curiosity, surprise and other strong emotions. This may be the reason why at different times you may love or hate your writing tasks. Staying aware of the emotional as well as the cognitive requirements associated with writing can help you to be more self aware about the nature of your own development as a writer.

### A person's sense of audience has a big effect on their writing and how they engage in writing tasks

It is usually easier to write when we write for a safe audience. You should try to think about your audience but you should also take time **not** to think about audience – to put audience out of your mind, particularly in the early stages of a writing task when your ideas feel fragile and you may need your own space and reflections to build and strengthen your voice. When your writing goes only to your tutor/lecturer and only for assessment, it can make all your writing feel 'high stakes'. Try to get their views and ideas on what you have written. See how much that experience can help to nourish and develop your writing skills and orientations.

---

**Chapter summary: Key learning points**

- Be aware that many students find writing very stressful, but there are simple ways to overcome the fears that it might create for you.
- Create safe spaces for yourself; try freewriting and outlining.
- Get used to drafting and redrafting: this really helps to improve your writing processes and outcomes.
- Take your audience into account – but not all the time, and not always at the beginning of your writing task, when basic ideas and concepts may be more important for you to grapple with.
- Practise your academic writing as often as possible, and make sure you are clear about what the features of academic writing generally are (see Table 6.1).

---

### Suggested further reading

Elbow, P. (1998) *Writing with Power: Techniques for Mastering the Writing Process*. Oxford: Oxford University Press.

Elbow, P. (2000) *Everyone Can Write*. Oxford: Oxford University Press.

# 7

# Learning the Rules: Punctuation, spelling, accurate referencing and avoiding plagiarism

## Chapter Contents

## Chapter Overview

- **Developing an active approach to help you gain confidence in the purpose and practice of good grammar**
- **Practising good use of punctuation, especially commas and apostrophes**
- **Exploring helpful spelling, referencing and citation conventions**
- **Avoiding plagiarism**

## Introduction

When it comes to learning the rules of the game for punctuation, spelling, referencing and avoiding plagiarism, the best way to learn is to do it. This chapter presents you with a range of exercises on these topics. There are ten exercises in total: four on English usage, four on referencing practice, and two on identifying plagiarism. Comments on and answers for all of these can be found towards the end of the chapter (pp. 119–128). If you feel after completing these, and checking your results, that you need to develop your skills and knowledge in these areas, some additional learning resources are suggested at the end of the chapter.

## Why bother?

Why bother? There are good, practical reasons why you should develop your skills in English and referencing. Accurate spelling and good sentence construction are essential parts of effective communication. If you understand and apply the rules, you will gain more confidence in your writing ability and enhance your credibility with others, including your tutors and potential employers.

Accurate referencing enhances your authority as a writer and steers you away from plagiarism. Referencing your sources accurately indicates to your tutors that you have researched the assignment topic; it properly acknowledges the hard work of the original authors; and it helps other people to locate the same sources for their own learning purposes. It also strengthens your own voice in assignments, as you can use sources to support your own ideas or arguments.

## Parts of speech

Before you start it is important to know about the key parts of speech in the English language. This understanding will help you with the rules of spelling and punctuation. You probably learned these rules at school or college, so this is just a quick reminder for you of verbs, nouns, pronouns, adjectives, adverbs, conjunctions and prepositions:

- **Verbs**: action or doing words, for example, 'Before you *start* it is important to *know* about parts of speech in the English language' (*start and know* are the verbs).
- **Nouns**: words which refer to a person, place, tangible thing, action, or an intangible state. *Common nouns* do not have capital letters, unless they begin a sentence. *Proper nouns* refer to one particular object, person, title, or place and always start with a capital letter. Examples of common nouns are woman, man, girl, boy, home, town, car, earth, wind, fire, honesty, love, hate, hope. Examples of proper nouns are The Dome, The Queen of England, Hamlet, The Lord of the Rings, The Olympic Games in London, Zak, John, Megan.
- **Pronouns**: used in place of a noun to avoid word repetition. These can be *personal pronouns* (I, me, you), *possessive pronouns* (my, mine, yours) or *relative* to the noun (which, that, who).
- **Adjectives**: give you more information about nouns or pronouns. For example: 'Jo is an *honest* person' or 'The opening ceremony of the Olympic Games was *spectacular*'.

- **Adverbs** (meaning 'added word'): tell you more about a verb, an adjective or another adverb. They tell you how, when or where something happened, is happening, or will happen, e.g. *soon, easily, only, there*. For example: 'The hawk swooped *silently* on its prey'.
- **Conjunctions**: join words, e.g. *and, or, but, that, because*.
- **Prepositions**: are used before a noun or pronoun to indicate place (*below, behind*) or position (*among, in*) or time (*after, until*). For example: 'The car slowed *at* the junction and then speeded *along* the dual carriageway *until* it reached the bridge'.

### Punctuation and spelling

The use or misuse of the comma is a common problem in student assignments. Commas act like pauses in the spoken word. They separate parts of a sentence and help the reader to make sense of what has been written.

---

*Exercise 7.1: Comma confusion*

Where do the commas go in the following sentences?

1    Two thieves one male armed with a handgun the other female armed with a knife audaciously robbed a bank at 10am yesterday on Bingley High Street West Yorkshire and stole £80,000.
2    Punctuation marks are like traffic signals. They guide readers they tell readers when to go and when to stop and when to turn and in what direction.
3    I asked for Jack Ashley's student records but received the file of Jack Ashton by mistake.
4    My daughter Chris will accompany me to the degree show tomorrow.
5    Meena has had an interesting challenging career so far.
6    The test of good writing is to read it aloud. If it sounds formal but still natural you have probably got the style and tone right although you would need to check the accuracy of the grammar and spelling.
7    Proofreading your own work is often difficult because for the most part you read what you thought you wrote.
8    Laura Wilson has been appointed to lead the Women's Engineering Forum in the department to take effect from 1 September.
9    If you have to write something critical try to phrase it in a way that will not be wounding to the other person.
10   As you probably know these models are considered to be top of the range.
11   Jack Lewis a student in your department has reported being unhappy with his marks for the last assignment.
12   To avoid misunderstanding and achieve effective results keep your sentences short.

---

## Exercise 7.2: Right or wrong?

Look at each of the following sentences. Decide which are correctly written and which contain errors of spelling and/or punctuation. Tick or put a cross in the appropriate column and underline any errors that you spot.

| Sentence: right or wrong? | ✓ if correct | ✗ if wrong |
|---|---|---|
| I wasn't sure whether to laugh or to cry. | | |
| My sister liked to make sure all her video's where in alphabetical order. | | |
| It's hot today, so it's a good job I brought that sun-cream from the chemist yesterday; it was on special offer. | | |
| Your requested to remove your muddy footware before entering the lounge. | | |
| IT Advise will be available from 10:00 to 12:00 today. | | |
| I'm sometimes too independent for my own good. | | |
| The noise effected my concentration. | | |
| I through a party for my friends last week. | | |
| They say there cheque is in the post. | | |
| There is a draft coming through that window. | | |
| We didn't no that an order had been sent. | | |
| I switched of the computer when I finished working. | | |
| The university accomodation is noisy but preferable to living on your own in some bedset. | | |
| There is an old saying that, 'a little knowlege is a dangerous thing'. | | |

## Proof-reading

Proof-reading is an essential element in effective writing. It is easy to miss errors in one's own work, particularly when working under time pressures. It is, therefore, a good idea to ask someone to check your assignment for spelling, grammatical, and sentence construction errors. There are professional proof-readers who will, for an agreed fee, check your work (see the exercise that follows); or you could ask someone with a good command of English to read it.

### Exercise 7.3: Proof-reading

A number of spelling and punctuation errors appear in the following short extract. Underline all the mistakes that you spot.

> Proof-reading includes checking text for spelling mistakes and gramatical errors. A proof-reader will always highlight errors but will leave the final decision about changing the text to you.
>
> A professionnal proof-reader should never attempt or pursuade you to change your ideas or style of writing you should retain ownership of your ideas and way of expressing them at all times.
>
> This is important as to avoid plagarism the work submited should be yours written by you and in your own words.
>
> However as suggested earlier a proof-reader will point out spelling and gramatical errors. If you make a note of these it can help you to improve your English and be an important part of the process of learning.

### British and US spellings

There are differences of spelling with some words between British and US English. If you are studying in an institution that requires British spellings, it is important to use these consistently in your assignments.

### Exercise 7.4: British and US spellings

Look at each of the following pairs of words and decide for each which is the British and which is the US spelling.

| | | |
|---|---|---|
| **Aging** (British/US) | **Colour** (British/US) | **Labor** (British/US) |
| **Ageing** (British/US) | **Color** (British/US) | **Labour** (British/US) |
| | | |
| **Analyse** (British/US) | **Favorite** (British/US) | **Program** (British/US) |
| **Analyze** (British/US) | **Favourite** (British/US) | **Programme** (British/US) |
| | | |
| **Catalogue** (British/US) | **Honor** (British/US) | **Skilful** (British/US) |
| **Catalog** (British/US) | **Honour** (British/US) | **Skillful** (British/US) |
| | | |
| **Centre** (British/US) | **Jewelry** (British/US) | **Traveller** (British/US) |
| **Center** (British/US) | **Jewellery** (British/US) | **Traveler** (British/US) |

## Referencing

With referencing, two things are expected of you:

- that you learn **when** you should reference sources – and when it is not necessary.
- that you learn **how** to reference in the referencing style adopted by your institution or department.

### *When to reference*

Referencing your sources of evidence is an important element in writing assignments, for the following reasons:

- To support your arguments and give credibility to the information and evidence presented.
- To enable others to find the sources you cite and to use the same evidence for their own purposes.
- To enable tutors and others to check the accuracy and validity of the evidence you have presented.
- To give an appreciation to originators of work for their contribution to knowledge.
- To demonstrate the range of your reading.
- To avoid plagiarism.

### *How to reference*

The rules governing how to reference are laid out in the different referencing styles to be found within UK higher education institutions, and you should adopt and learn the style required by your course. Although there are at least fourteen separate referencing styles in active use within Britain, they can be broken into two main groups: name referencing and number referencing.

### *Name referencing*

Name referencing involves using the surname or family name of the author(s) or name of originator in the main text of the assignment, along with the year of publication and the page number, if it is a printed source. This is called a **citation**.

The citation connects with the full details of the source in an alphabetical list ('References' or 'Bibliography') at the end of the assignment.

The main referencing styles that use this system are as follows:

- Name-date (Harvard) style.
- APA (American Psychological Association) style.
- MLA (Modern Language Association) style.

### Number referencing

Number referencing involves the use of consecutive or recurrent superscripts or bracketed numbers in the main text of an assignment. These connect with the full details of the source in either footnotes or endnotes.

The main referencing styles that use this system are as follows:

- Styles using consecutive numbers:
  - British Standard (Running Notes) style.
  - MHRA (Modern Humanities Research Association) style.
  - Chicago (or Turabian) style.
  - OSCOLA (Oxford Standard for Citation of Legal Authorities) style.
- Styles using recurrent numbers:
  - British Standard (Numeric) style.
  - Vancouver style.
  - IEEE (Institute of Electrical and Electronics Engineers) style.
  - CSE (Council of Science Editors) style.

Referencing styles are often linked to professional associations. For example, psychologists often use the APA style because of its origins with the American Psychological Association, while many engineering departments in Britain and elsewhere use the IEEE style, as developed and recommended by the Institute of Electrical and Electronics Engineers. However, despite the number of referencing styles in use in Britain, the name-date **(Harvard)** style is the one that has been adopted by a significant number of departments within UK higher education institutions (Neville 2007: 43).

### Name-date (Harvard) style

The basic idea of the name-date (Harvard) style is as follows:

- In the text of an assignment, cite the surname or family name of the author(s) or the organizational name, plus the year of publication.
- List all the cited references in full, and in alphabetical order, at the end of the assignment.
- Ensure that the names and dates used in the citation connect with the names and dates used in the full reference entry.

Thus in the text you give a partial reference (a **citation**). This is the last name of the originator, followed by the year of publication. An originator can be the author(s) or the name of an organization, including website names. Lengthy names of organizations can be abbreviated, providing you explain the citation in the full reference, as in the example that follows – (YHES 1998). The citations in the following paragraph are shown in **bold**, although you would not normally do this in an assignment.

Although **Handy (1994)** has argued that education is the key to economic success for individuals, organizations and nations, a majority of adults in the UK have yet to be convinced or persuaded of this argument. In 1999 only forty per cent of adults had participated in any sort of formal learning in the previous three years. Of these, a significant majority was from social class groups A, B and C. Only a quarter of adults from semi-skilled or unskilled work backgrounds had involved themselves in formal education **(Tuckett 1999)**. The consequences for people without qualifications who lose their jobs are often serious. A study of long-term unemployed people in Yorkshire found that sixty-one per cent had no educational qualifications, and a significant number of these had special learning needs **(YHES 1998)**. There would appear to be a link too, between lack of qualifications, poor health and a disengagement from participation in political or civic life, and which could aggravate the situation of unemployment for the people concerned **(Hagen 2002)**.

(Taken from Neville 2007: 51)

The full list of references at the end of the assignment for just these four citations would look as follows:

## References

Hagen, J. (2002) *Basic Skills for Adults.* Birmingham: Guidance Council.
Handy, C. (1994) *The Empty Raincoat: Making Sense of the Future.* London: Hutchinson.
Tuckett, A. (1999) 'Who's learning what?' *Guardian*, 18 May, p. 13.
YHES (Yorkshire and Humber Employment Service) (1998) *Survey of Clients Aged 25+ Unemployed for Two Years or More* [Report]. London: Department for Education and Employment.

References include, usually in the following order, this basic information:

- The family name, followed by the initials (or personal name) of the author(s).
- The year of publication of the source.
- The title of the main source – in italics or underlined – and edition number, if relevant.
- The place of publication, followed by name of publisher.

References can also include the following:

- Names of editor(s) in an edited book.
- Title of an edited book.
- Full website URL or Digital Object Identifier information.
- Volume, issue and page numbers for journal articles.

> **Key tip**
>
> If you include more than one reference to the same named author, these are entered in chronological order.

Referencing your sources properly is an important protection for you against accusations of plagiarism. The exercises that follow cover both the elements of successful referencing practice, and how to avoid plagiarism.

> ### Exercise 7.5:  Is a reference needed?
>
> When is a reference necessary in an assignment? Decide if a reference to a source is needed in the following situations, and tick either 'Yes' or 'No'.
>
> | Situation | Yes | No |
> |---|---|---|
> | 1   When quoting directly from a published source. | | |
> | 2   When using statistics or other data that are freely available from a publicly accessible website. | | |
> | 3   When summarizing the cause of undisputed past events and where there is agreement by most commentators on cause and effect. | | |
> | 4   When paraphrasing a definition found on a website and when no writer, editor or author's name is shown. | | |
> | 5   When summarizing or paraphrasing the ideas of a key commentator or author, but taken from a secondary source, e.g. general reference book. | | |
> | 6   When summarizing in a concluding paragraph of your assignment what you have discussed and referenced earlier in your text. | | |
> | 7   When including in your assignment photographs or graphics that are freely available on the Internet and where no named photographer or originator is shown. | | |
> | 8   When emphasizing an idea you have read that you feel makes an important contribution to the points made in your assignment. | | |
> | 9   When summarizing undisputed and commonplace facts about the world. | | |

### Where should the citations go?

Citations are the names or numbers that you place into the text of your assignment to identify the source of evidence presented. For example, and as shown earlier, in the name-date (Harvard) referencing style, the citations used are the surnames of authors or originators of the source in question, followed by the year of its publication, e.g. (Handy 1994). These citations should connect with the full detail of the source contained in the alphabetical list of references at the end of the assignment. For example, the following essay paragraph contains two citations that help the reader to identify the source of the definition used (i.e. Coleman and Chiva 1991) and the hypothesis presented (i.e. Hopson and Scaly 1999).

> Life planning is a process to encourage people to review their lives, identify life priorities, consider options and make plans to implement choices (Coleman and Chiva 1991). It is an idea that started in the USA, but has found its way to Britain and the rest of Europe in recent years. Hopson and Scally (1999) suggest the process is built on seven life management skills: knowing yourself; learning from experience; research and information retrieval skills; setting objectives and making action plans; making decisions; looking after yourself; and communicating with others. They argue that these skills are necessary to avoid 'pinball living': where individuals are bounced from one situation to another without any clear direction.

### Exercise 7.6: Where should citations be inserted?

Look at the following three brief extracts from assignments and decide if a citation is necessary, and if so, where it should go. Mark every relevant point in the text with **X**.

1   A major study of British school leavers concluded that parents had a major influence on the kind of work entered by their children. The children were influenced over a long period of time by the values and ideas about work of their parents. A later study reached the same conclusion, and showed a link between the social and economic status of parents and the work attitudes and aspirations of their teenage children.
2   Climatologists generally agree that the five warmest years since the late nineteenth century have been within the decade 1995–2005, with the National Oceanic and Atmospheric Administration (NOAA) and the World Meteorological Organization (WMO) ranking 2005 as the second warmest year behind 1998.
3   It has been argued that federalism is a way of making sense of large organizations and that the power and responsibility that drives federalism is a feature of developed societies and can be extended into a way forward for managing modern business because 'it has been designed to create a balance of power within an institution. It matches paradox with paradox'.

**Exercise 7.7: 'I didn't reference the source because . . .'**

Below are six statements that might be made by some students for not referencing a particular source in the text of an assignment. They all start with '*I didn't reference the source because* . . .' However, what would, or might, you say in response to counter these statements? Six likely responses are shown. Match the likely response to the statement. Write the most likely response number in the right-hand column below.

| Statements | Response number |
|---|---|
| I didn't reference the source in the text of the assignment because I put the source in the bibliography. | |
| I didn't reference the source because I found this theory on a Wiki Internet site; anyone can contribute to these, and no particular author is named. | |
| I didn't reference the source because the statistics were taken from a government website - there for the whole world to see and use. | |
| I didn't reference the source because it just gave me ideas to use in my assignment; I changed most words in the article to my own. | |
| I didn't reference the source of the definition because it was from a tutor handout; everyone in class was given a copy. | |
| I didn't reference the source because no author or writer's name was shown on the website. | |

*Responses*

Match each of the previous statements with an appropriate counter-response from the list below.

1  If no named author or writer is shown, you should cite and reference the name of the originator of the source, which can be the name of an organization or other source.
2  Readers need to match in-text citations with the full details of sources in a list of references. This enables readers to find and use the sources for themselves, if required.
3  The source of all data like these must be fully referenced. Readers may, for example, want to learn or examine the methodology for the research and data collection.
4  It is advisable, wherever possible, to use primary sources in an assignment, rather than secondary sources. A primary source, in this example, would be the originator of the theory. Secondary sources may not always be reliable. However, if you do use a secondary source, it needs to be properly referenced.
5  Any source that has played a significant contribution to your assignment must be fully referenced. By doing this you acknowledge the part another person has played in the development of your own ideas.

6 This came from work produced by someone else and not by you. It also contributes to the reader's understanding of terms you have used in your assignment and so needs to be properly referenced.

---

### Exercise 7.8: *Referencing errors?*

Remind yourself, from the information presented earlier in this chapter, what information is required in a full reference entry and then look at the sources presented below. Identify and summarize in the right-hand column the nature of any errors that you spot.

| References | Error(s)? |
|---|---|
| *www.bbc.co.uk/bob/callcentres/* [Accessed 09/08/2004]. | |
| Business Strategies (2000) *Tomorrow's Call Centres: A Research Study.* | |
| Department for Trade and Industry (2004) *The UK Contact Centre Industry: A Study.* [Report]. London: Department for Trade and Industry. | |
| Health and Safety executive. *Psychosocial Working Conditions in Great Britain in 2004.* | |
| Huws, U. (1999) *Virtually There: the Evolution of Call Centres.* [Report]. London: Mitel Telecom Ltd. | |
| Huws, U. (1993) *Teleworking in Britain: A Report to the Employment Department.* Research Series No 18, Oct 1993. London: Department of Employment. | |
| Huws, U. (1996) *eWorking: An Overview of the Research.* [Report]. London: Department of Trade and Industry. | |

---

## Plagiarism

Plagiarism is a term used to describe a practice that involves knowingly taking and using another person's **work** and claiming it, directly or indirectly, as your own. This is work that must have been made accessible to others in a tangible way, e.g. written in printed or electronic forms, or performed, or presented visually and/or orally to others.

### Exercise 7.9: Is it plagiarism?

Which of these scenarios do you think would be regarded as plagiarism by most institutions of higher education in Britain? Tick either 'Yes' or 'No'.

| Scenario | Yes | No |
| --- | --- | --- |
| 1   You see a useful article on an Internet site that will be helpful in your assignment. You copy 40 per cent of the words from this source, and substitute 60 per cent of your own words. You don't include a source, as no author's name is shown on the site. | | |
| 2   You summarize a point taken from a course handout given to you by your tutor that contains secondary information, i.e. the tutor has presented an overview of the work of others. You do not reference the handout, as it has not been published outside the university and is just for the limited use of the students on the course. | | |
| 3   You are part of a study group of six students. An individual essay assignment has been set by a tutor. Each member of the group researches and writes a section of the essay. The work is collated and written by one student and all the group members individually submit this collective and collated work. | | |
| 4   You include the expression 'An apple a day keeps the doctor away' in your essay without a reference to a source. | | |
| 5   You discuss an essay assignment with a classmate. She has some interesting ideas and perspectives on the topic, which you use in your essay. But no reference to your classmate and her ideas are included in your essay. | | |
| 6   Your command of written English is not as good as you would like it to be. You explain to another student what you want to say in an essay. The student writes it on your behalf, and you then submit it. | | |

### Exercise 7.10: More plagiarism?

Read the following extract from a book on referencing (Neville 2007: 8). Then look at the four examples that attempt to transfer the information from the extract into assignments. Decide which, if any of these, amount to plagiarism.

*Original extract*

Academic study involves not just presenting and describing ideas, but also being aware of where they came from, who developed them, why, and when. The 'when' is particularly important. Ideas, models, theories and practices originate from somewhere and someone. These are often shaped by the social norms and practices prevailing at the time and place of their origin and the student in Higher Education needs to be aware of these influences. Referencing, therefore, plays an important role in helping to locate and place ideas and arguments in their historical, social, cultural and geographical contexts.

**Source**: Neville, C. (2007) *The Complete Guide to Referencing and Avoiding Plagiarism.* Maidenhead: Open University Press.

Decide which, if any of the following, amount to plagiarism.

*Example 1*

Academic study involves presenting and describing ideas and being aware of where they came from, who developed them, when, and why. Knowing when to reference is particularly important as ideas, models, theories and practices originate from somewhere and someone. These are often moulded by the social norms and practices prevailing at the time and place of their origin and students on degree courses need to be aware of these influences. It can be said then that referencing plays an important role in helping to locate and place ideas and arguments in their historical, social, cultural and geographical contexts.

**Is this plagiarism?** **Yes** ☐ **No** ☐

*Example 2*

Academic study involves not just presenting and describing ideas, but also being aware of where they came from, who developed them, why, and when. The 'when' is particularly important. Ideas, models, theories and practices originate from somewhere and someone. These are often shaped by the social norms and practices prevailing at the time and place of their origin and the student in Higher Education needs to be aware of these influences. Referencing, therefore, plays an important role in helping to locate and place ideas and arguments into their historical, social, cultural and geographical contexts (Neville 2007).

**Is this plagiarism?** **Yes** ☐ **No** ☐

*Example 3*

Neville (2007) has argued that referencing can help a scholar to trace a path back to the origin of ideas. Ideas do not develop in a vacuum, but are formed by social, historical, economic and other factors. Referencing is important then, not just for identifying who said something, but when and why they said it.

**Is this plagiarism?** **Yes** ☐ **No** ☐

*Example 4*

Academic study involves not just presenting and describing ideas, but also being aware of where they came from, who developed them, why, and when. It can be argued that the 'when' is particularly important because ideas, models, theories and practices originate from somewhere and someone. Neville (2007) has suggested that:

> *These are often shaped by the social norms and practices prevailing at the time and place of their origin and the student in Higher Education needs to be aware of these influences.*

(Neville 2007: 8)

So referencing plays an important role in helping to locate and place ideas and arguments in their historical, social, cultural and geographical contexts.

**Is this plagiarism?    Yes ☐   No ☐**

## Comments on and answers to the exercises in this chapter

This section provides comments on and answers to the exercises you may have attempted earlier in this chapter.

### Exercise 7.1: Comma confusion

1  Two thieves, one male armed with a handgun, the other female armed with a knife, audaciously robbed a bank at 10am yesterday on Bingley High Street, West Yorkshire, and stole £80,000.
2  Punctuation marks are like traffic signals. They guide readers, they tell readers when to go and when to stop, and when to turn and in what direction.
3  I asked for Jack Ashley's student records, but received the file of Jack Ashton by mistake.
4  My daughter, Chris, will accompany me to the degree show tomorrow.
5  Meena has had an interesting, challenging career so far.
6  The test of good writing is to read it aloud. If it sounds formal, but still natural, you have probably got the style and tone right, although you would need to check the accuracy of the grammar and spelling.
7  Proofreading your own work is often difficult because, for the most part, you read what you thought you wrote.
8  Laura Wilson has been appointed to lead the Women's Engineering Forum in the department, to take effect from 1 September.
9  If you have to write something critical, try to phrase it in a way that will not be wounding to the other person.
10  As you probably know, these models are considered to be top of the range.
11  Jack Lewis, a student in your department, has reported being unhappy with his marks for the last assignment.
12  To avoid misunderstanding and achieve effective results, keep your sentences short.

## Exercise 7.2: *Right or wrong?*

Errors are shown below in bold, followed by our comments.

| Sentence: right or wrong? | ✓ if correct | ✗ if wrong |
|---|:---:|:---:|
| I wasn't sure whether to laugh or to cry. | ✓ | |
| My sister liked to make sure all her **video's where** in alphabetical order.<br>**Comment**: *There is no apostrophe in 'videos', as it refers to the plural use of the word; also, the correct word to use is 'were' (describing a state) and not 'where' (indicating a place).* | | ✗ |
| It's hot today, so it's a good job I **brought** that sun-cream from the chemist yesterday; it was on special offer.<br>**Comment**: *The correct verb to use is 'bought' (to buy), not 'brought' (to bring).* | | ✗ |
| **Your** requested to remove your muddy **footware** before entering the lounge.<br>**Comment**: *The notice contains two errors. It should read '**You are** requested to remove your muddy **footwear** before entering the lounge.' However, 'You are' could be abbreviated to 'You're' by use of an apostrophe.* | | ✗ |
| IT **Advise** will be available from 10:00 to 12:00 today.<br>**Comment**: *The correct word to use is 'advice', a noun, and not the verb 'advise'. There is a useful rhyme to help you to remember this rule: '**S** is the verb and **C** is the noun. That's the rule that runs the town' (Parkinson 2007).* | | ✗ |
| I'm sometimes too independent for my own good. | ✓ | |
| The noise **effected** my concentration.<br>**Comment**: *The correct word to use is the verb 'affected'. The **E** (effected) is used when the word is a noun. The sentence could have used both words, e.g. The **effect** of the noise **affected** my concentration.* | | ✗ |
| I **through** a party for my friends last week.<br>**Comment**: *The correct word to use is the verb 'threw', not the preposition 'through'.* | | ✗ |
| They say **there** cheque is in the post.<br>**Comment**: *The correct word to use is the adjective 'their' (belonging to them) and not the adverb 'there', which relates to place.* | | ✗ |
| There is a **draft** coming through that window.<br>**Comment**: *The correct noun to use in this context is 'draught', not 'draft' (which means a preliminary version, as in a draft essay). Watch out for words which have the same sound, but different spelling according to the context.* | | ✗ |
| We **did'nt no** that an order had been sent.<br>**Comment**: *The apostrophe needs to be placed after the letter 'n', i.e. 'didn't', and the correct word to use is the verb 'know', and not 'no'.* | | ✗ |
| I switched **of** the computer when I finished working.<br>**Comment**: *The correct word to use is the adverb 'off', not the preposition 'of'.* | | ✗ |

| The university **accomodation** is noisy**,** but preferable to living on your own in some **bedset**.<br>**Comment**: *The correct spelling is 'accommodation', a comma should be used after 'noisy', and the correct word is 'bedsit', not 'bedset'.* | | ✗ |
| There is an old saying that, 'a little **knowlege** is a dangerous thing'.<br>**Comment**: *The word is spelt 'knowledge' – this is a very common spelling error.* | | ✗ |

## Exercise 7.3: Proof-reading

The changes made are highlighted in **bold**, including the relevant punctuation.

Proof-reading includes checking text for spelling mistakes and **grammatical** errors. A proof-reader will always highlight errors, but will leave the final decision about changing the text to you.

A **professional** proof-reader should never attempt or **persuade** you to change your ideas or style of writing; you should retain ownership of your ideas and way of expressing them at all times.

This is important, as to avoid **plagiarism** the work **submitted** should be yours, written by you, and in your own words.

However, as suggested earlier, a proof-reader will point out spelling and **grammatical** errors. If you make a note of these, it can help you to improve your English and be an important part of the process of learning.

## Exercise 7.4: British and US spellings

**Aging** (US)  
**Ageing** (British)

**Colour** (British)  
**Color** (US)

**Labor** (US)  
**Labour** (British)

**Analyse** (British)  
**Analyze** (US)

**Favorite** (US)  
**Favourite** (British)

**Program** (US)  
**Programme** (British)

**Catalogue** (British)  
**Catalog** (US)

**Honor** (US)  
**Honour** (British)

**Skilful** (British)  
**Skillful** (US)

**Centre** (British)  
**Center** (US)

**Jewelry** (US)  
**Jewellery** (British)

**Traveller** (British)  
**Traveler** (US)

*Exercise 7.5:  Is a reference needed?*

| Situation | Yes | No |
|---|---|---|
| 1   When quoting directly from a published source.<br>**Comment**: *The sources of all quotations should be referenced.* | ✓ | |
| 2   When using statistics or other data that are freely available from a publicly accessible website.<br>**Comment**: *The sources of statistics or other data that you use in assignments should always be referenced.* | ✓ | |
| 3   When summarizing the cause of undisputed past events and where there is agreement by most commentators on cause and effect.<br>**Comment**: *This can be regarded as common knowledge, which does not need to be referenced. However, the sources for any contentious discussion of the same events would need to referenced.* | | ✓ |
| 4   When paraphrasing a definition found on a website and when no writer, editor or author's name is shown.<br>**Comment**: *If no named writer, author or editor is shown, you should cite and reference the name of the website, e.g. Bized 2007.* | ✓ | |
| 5   When summarizing or paraphrasing the ideas of a key commentator or author, but taken from a secondary source, e.g. general reference book.<br>**Comment**: *You always need to acknowledge your sources, even if they are secondary ones. However, it is advisable, whenever possible, to consult the main (primary) sources for yourself and to reference these.* | ✓ | |
| 6   When summarizing in a concluding paragraph of your assignment what you have discussed and referenced earlier in your text.<br>**Comment**: *Providing the sources were properly referenced earlier in your assignment, there would be no need to re-reference your concluding comments. However, any new material introduced into your assignment at this point would need to be referenced.* | | ✓ |
| 7   When including in your assignment photographs or graphics that are freely available on the Internet and where no named photographer or originator is shown.<br>**Comment**: *The photographs or graphics are the result of work by another person. In this situation you should cite and reference the name of the website that contains the illustrations.* | ✓ | |
| 8   When emphasizing an idea you have read that you feel makes an important contribution to the points made in your assignment.<br>**Comment**: *This is a crucial reason for referencing, as it acknowledges the significance and relevance of the source concerned to the development of your own work.* | ✓ | |
| 9   When summarizing undisputed and commonplace facts about the world.<br>**Comment**: *General public awareness of undisputed facts can also be treated as common knowledge (see also Comment 3, above).* | | ✓ |

### Exercise 7.6: Where should citations be inserted?

1   A major study of British school leavers concluded that parents had a major influence on the kind of work entered by their children **X**. The children were influenced over a long period of time by the values and ideas about work of their parents. A later study reached the same conclusion, and showed a link between the social and economic status of parents and the work attitudes and aspirations of their teenage children **X**.

   *Comment: The above extract refers to **two** different studies, so you need to cite both of these. You have some flexibility about where the citations should go. For example, the relevant citations could also have been placed after the words 'study' in lines 1 and 4. The important point is to make the connection between statement and source as obvious and clear as possible.*

2   Climatologists generally agree that the five warmest years since the late nineteenth century have been within the decade 1995–2005, with the National Oceanic and Atmospheric Administration (NOAA) and the World Meteorological Organization (WMO) ranking 2005 as the second warmest year behind 1998 **X**.

   *Comment: The sources of all statistics and information originating from named sources, such as the NOAA and WMO, should always be fully referenced.*

3   It has been argued that federalism is a way of making sense of large organizations and that the power and responsibility that drives federalism is a feature of developed societies and can be extended into a way forward for managing modern business because 'it has been designed to create a balance of power within an institution. It matches paradox with paradox' **X**.

   *Comment: If you use the term, 'It has been argued . . .', you need to cite **who** has presented this argument. As a quotation is included, you can show the source of the argument and quotation – assuming they are from the same source – immediately after the quotation. If the quotation is taken from a printed source, show the page number, as well as the author's name and year of publication, as this helps others to easily locate the quotation in the source cited, e.g. (Handy 1994: 98).*

**Note**: As mentioned earlier in this chapter, the Handy (1994) citation would connect with the full details of the source in a list of references. So the full reference for the citation example shown would look like this:

Handy, C. (1994) *The Empty Raincoat: Making Sense of the Future.* London: Hutchinson.

*Exercise 7.7: 'I didn't reference the source because...'*

| Statements | Response number |
|---|---|
| I didn't reference the source in the text of the assignment because I put the source in the bibliography. | **2** *Readers need to match in-text citations with the full details of sources in a list of references. This enables readers to find and use the sources for themselves, if required.* |
| I didn't reference the source because I found this theory on a Wiki Internet site; anyone can contribute to these, and no particular author is named. | **4** *It is advisable, wherever possible, to use primary sources in an assignment, rather than secondary sources. A primary source, in this example, would be the originator of the theory. Secondary sources may not always be reliable. However, if you do use a secondary source, it needs to be properly referenced.* |
| I didn't reference the source because the statistics were taken from a government website – there for the whole world to see and use. | **3** *The source of all data like these must be fully referenced. Readers may, for example, want to learn or examine the methodology for the research and data collection.* |
| I didn't reference the source because it just gave me ideas to use in my assignment; I changed most of words in the article to my own. | **5** *Any source that has played a significant contribution to your assignment must be fully referenced. By doing this you acknowledge the part another person has played in the development of your own ideas.* |
| I didn't reference the source of the definition because it was from a tutor handout; everyone in class was given a copy. | **6** *This came from work produced by someone else and not by you. It also contributes to the reader's understanding of terms you have used in your assignment and so needs to be properly referenced.* |
| I didn't reference the source because no author or writer's name was shown on the website. | **1** *If no named author or writer is shown, you should cite and reference the name of the originator of the source, which can be the name of an organization or other source.* |

**Exercise 7.8: Referencing errors?**

*Http://www.bbc.co.uk/bob/callcentres/* [Accessed 09/08/2004].
**Comment**: More information is needed; in this example, the name of author or originator and title of item needed to be shown, e.g. BBC (2004) *Brassed-off Britain: Call Centres*. Available at **www.bbc.co.uk/bob/callcentres/** [Accessed 09/08/2004].

Business Strategies (2000) *Tomorrow's Call Centres: A Research Study.*
**Comment**: You need to give details of where this study can be located, e.g. name of publisher or details of website, e.g. Business Strategies (2000) *Tomorrow's Call Centres: A Research Study*. Available at **www.businessstrategies.co.uk** [Accessed 07/07/2008].

Department for Trade and Industry (2004) *The UK Contact Centre Industry: A Study*. [Report]. London: Department for Trade and Industry.
**Comment**: This source is correctly referenced.

Health and Safety Executive. *Psychosocial Working Conditions in Great Britain in 2004.*
**Comment**: The date of publication and details of the publisher are missing. If the text is anything other than a book, you need to state what it is, e.g. a report. So the full reference should look like this: Health and Safety Executive (2004) *Psychosocial Working Conditions in Great Britain in 2004.* [Report]. London: Health and Safety Executive.

**Huws, U.** (1999) *Virtually There: the Evolution of Call Centres*. [Report]. London: Mitel Telecom Ltd.
**Huws, U.** (1993) *Teleworking in Britain: A Report to the Employment Department.* Research Series No 18, Oct 1993. London: Department of Employment.
**Huws, U.** (1996) *eWorking: An Overview of the Research*. [Report]. London: Department of Trade and Industry.
**Comment**: Where you have more than one publication by the same author these need to be listed in chronological order, with the earliest source listed first. So Huws (1993) would be the first listed of the three shown here, then Huws (1996) and Huws (1999).

## Exercise 7.9: Is it plagiarism?

| Scenario | Yes | No |
|---|---|---|
| 1 You see a useful article on an Internet site that will be helpful in your assignment. You copy 40 per cent of the words from this source and substitute 60 per cent of your own words. You don't include a source, as no author's name is shown on the site.<br>**Comment**: *You should always acknowledge the sources of items that have contributed to your own knowledge. If no author's name is shown, you should reference the name of the website. The point that you used 60 per cent of your own words in the process is irrelevant; you still need to acknowledge the source.* | ✓ | |
| 2 You summarize a point taken from a course handout given to you by your tutor that contains secondary information, i.e. the tutor has summarized the work of others. You do not reference the handout, as it has not been published outside the university and is just for the limited use of the students on the course.<br>**Comment**: *The handout is the result of work by your tutor and circulated to others, albeit a specialist readership. You need, therefore, to acknowledge the source in your assignment.* | ✓ | |
| 3 You are part of a study group of six students. An individual essay assignment has been set by a tutor. Each member of the group researches and writes a section of the essay. The work is collated and written by one student and all the group members individually submit this collective and collated work.<br>**Comment:** *Study groups are an excellent way to share and discuss ideas for assignments. But if an individual assignment has been set, then each member of the group must write his or her own version and interpretation of the group discussion and research.* | ✓ | |
| 4 You include the expression 'An apple a day keeps the doctor away' in your essay without a reference to a source.<br>**Comment**: *This is an example of a common expression, or aphorism which does not need to be referenced if the source or origin of the expression has been lost in the mist of time. The only exception to this might be if you were researching the origins of such expressions and needed to trace the development of them. If you were able to identify the period of origin of an expression, you could mention this, e.g. 'Children should be seen and not heard' (fifteenth-century British proverb).* | | ✓ |
| 5 You discuss an essay assignment with a classmate. She has some interesting ideas and perspectives on the topic, which you use in your essay. But no reference to your classmate and her ideas are included in your essay.<br>**Comment**: *Only tangible 'work', and not ideas, can be plagiarized. We are influenced by ideas all the time; this is how we learn. If, however, your classmate had made her ideas public, e.g. in an article, handout to the class, or in a formal lecture, then you would reference this. You could, however, acknowledge the contribution of your classmate in a preface at the start of your assignment, or in a note at the end. This would be good manners and an act of academic integrity.* | | ✓ |
| 6 Your command of written English is not as good as you would like it to be. You explain to another student what you want to say in an essay. The student writes it on your behalf and you then submit it.<br>**Comment**: *You must write this essay yourself. If you feel you need help with English, you should seek advice from the learning development services at your place of study.* | ✓ | |

## Exercise 7.10: More plagiarism?

*Original extract*

Academic study involves not just presenting and describing ideas, but also being aware of where they came from, who developed them, why, and when. The 'when' is particularly important. Ideas, models, theories and practices originate from somewhere and someone. These are often shaped by the social norms and practices prevailing at the time and place of their origin and the student in Higher Education needs to be aware of these influences. Referencing, therefore, plays an important role in helping to locate and place ideas and arguments in their historical, social, cultural and geographical contexts.

*Example 1*

Academic study involves presenting and describing ideas and being aware of where they came from, who developed them, when, and why. Knowing when to reference is particularly important as ideas, models, theories and practices originate from somewhere and someone. These are often moulded by the social norms and practices prevailing at the time and place of their origin and students on degree courses need to be aware of these influences. It can be said then that referencing plays an important role in helping to locate and place ideas and arguments in their historical, social, cultural and geographical contexts.

**Is this plagiarism? Yes.** It is almost identical to the original and there is no attempt to identify the source.

*Example 2*

Academic study involves not just presenting and describing ideas, but also being aware of where they came from, who developed them, why, and when. The 'when' is particularly important. Ideas, models, theories and practices originate from somewhere and someone. These are often shaped by the social norms and practices prevailing at the time and place of their origin and the student in Higher Education needs to be aware of these influences. Referencing, therefore, plays an important role in helping to locate and place ideas and arguments into their historical, social, cultural and geographical contexts (Neville 2007).

**Is this plagiarism? Yes.** Although the source is cited, the text has been directly copied into the assignment. This implies that the words have been written by the student concerned, which is clearly not the case. The student should have tried to paraphrase the original extract in his or her own words.

*Example 3*

Neville (2007) has argued that referencing can help a scholar to trace a path back to the origin of ideas. Ideas do not develop in a vacuum, but are formed by social, historical, economic and other factors. Referencing is important then, not just for identifying who said something, but when and why they said it.

**Is this plagiarism? No.** It is a good effort to paraphrase the original extract and to acknowledge the source.

*Example 4*

Academic study involves not just presenting and describing ideas, but also being aware of where they came from, who developed them, why, and when. It can be argued that the 'when' is particularly important because ideas, models, theories and practices originate from somewhere and someone. Neville (2007) has suggested that:

> *These are often shaped by the social norms and practices prevailing at the time and place of their origin and the student in Higher Education needs to be aware of these influences.*

(Neville 2007: 8)

So referencing plays an important role in helping to locate and place ideas and arguments in their historical, social, cultural and geographical contexts.

**Is this plagiarism? Yes.** The quotation used implies that the rest was written by the student, which is not the case. Even though the source is cited, most of the text is a direct copy from the original.

---

## Chapter summary: Key learning points

- Recognize that good grammar, punctuation and awareness of referencing rules are important.
- Be assured that there is nothing really mysterious about these conventions: once you learn the rules and practise them, they become easier – and just part of what you do when studying, researching and writing.
- Understand that avoiding plagiarism will help you to become a more confident learner with a strong notion of how your own ideas and knowledge relate to those of experts and writers in the field.

### Suggested further reading

#### English grammar, punctuation and spelling

Collinson, D., Kirkup, G., Kyd, R. and Slocombe, L. (1992) *Plain English*. Buckingham: Open University Press.

Peck, J. and Coyle, M. (2005) *The Student's Guide to Writing: Grammar, Punctuation and Spelling*. Basingstoke: Palgrave Macmillan.

Sinclair, C. (2007) *Grammar: A Friendly Approach*. Maidenhead: Open University Press.

Truss, L. (2003) *Eats, Shoots and Leaves: The Zero Tolerance Approach to Punctuation*. London: Profile Books.

#### Referencing

Neville, C. (2010) *The Complete Guide to Referencing and Avoiding Plagiarism*, 2nd edn. Maidenhead: Open University Press.

Pears, R. and Shields, G. (2008) *Cite Them Right: The Essential Guide to Referencing and Plagiarism*. Newcastle upon Tyne: Pear Tree Books.

# 8

# The Time of your Life: Managing time and living life as a student

## Chapter Contents

## Chapter Overview

- **Finding out more about your own orientation to managing time**
- **Recognizing time-related issues that can be problematic for students**
- **Planning, prioritizing, scheduling and delivering**
- **Developing some practical time management techniques**

## Introduction

Managing time is one of the biggest challenges students face. For younger students, a degree course may be the first time they have lived away from home and away from the support given by other people, particularly parents. They now have to juggle not only the demands of course work but also all other aspects of life, including laundry, cooking and part-time employment. For mature students, their studies may have to be managed alongside the responsibilities of running a home, being a parent, carer and employee; it is not easy.

Time management is a bit like dieting or exercise; you know you *should* be doing it, but put off starting, or soon give up. With time management, the half-hearted know they **should** have a plan, and that they **should** stick to it. But without strong motivation to succeed, they find it difficult to stick to any plan for too long.

So although this chapter will contain predictable stuff about time planning, it will also ask you to think about your attitudes to time, as attitudes can drive behaviour.

### Time management questionnaire

How well do you manage time? Try this **time management questionnaire**. Tick the response closest to your answer as follows: 0 for 'never', 1 for 'sometimes' and 2 for 'always'.

| | | | |
|---|---|---|---|
| I prioritze the things that need to be done. | 0 | 1 | 2 |
| I usually finish what I set out to do in any day. | 0 | 1 | 2 |
| In the past I have always got academic work done on time. | 0 | 1 | 2 |
| I feel I make the best use of my time. | 0 | 1 | 2 |
| I can tackle difficult or unpleasant tasks without using delaying tactics and wasting time. | 0 | 1 | 2 |
| I force myself to make time for planning. | 0 | 1 | 2 |
| I am spending enough time planning. | 0 | 1 | 2 |
| I prepare a daily or weekly list of tasks to be accomplished. | 0 | 1 | 2 |
| I prioritze my list in order of importance, not urgency (importance is what you want to do; urgent is what you have to do). | 0 | 1 | 2 |
| I am able to meet deadlines with time to spare. | 0 | 1 | 2 |
| I can usually keep up-to-date with my reading and course assignments. | 0 | 1 | 2 |
| I prevent interruptions from distracting me from high priority tasks. | 0 | 1 | 2 |
| I avoid spending too much time on things that divert me from what I should be doing. | 0 | 1 | 2 |
| I feel I spend enough time on course work. | 0 | 1 | 2 |

| | 0 | 1 | 2 |
|---|---|---|---|
| I plan time for relaxation in my weekly schedule. | 0 | 1 | 2 |
| I have a weekly schedule on which I record fixed commitments, such as lectures and tutorials. | 0 | 1 | 2 |
| I try to do the most important tasks during my peak energy periods of the day. | 0 | 1 | 2 |
| I make use of travel time to read course work. | 0 | 1 | 2 |
| I regularly reassess my activities in relation to my goals. | 0 | 1 | 2 |
| I have made a point of stopping activities that are wasting time. | 0 | 1 | 2 |
| I judge myself by the completion of tasks, rather than by the amount of activity spent on them. | 0 | 1 | 2 |
| I decide what needs to be done and am not controlled by events or what other people want me to do. | 0 | 1 | 2 |
| I have a clear idea of what I want to accomplish during the coming semester. | 0 | 1 | 2 |
| I am satisfied with the way I use my time. | 0 | 1 | 2 |
| I usually turn up on time for appointments and other commitments. | 0 | 1 | 2 |

**Your total score** ☐

## Scoring the questionnaire

**47–50 points**: You appear to be an excellent time manager. You may, however, be interested to read the remainder of this chapter to compare your own strategies with those suggested by the authors.

**38–46 points**: Generally you are a good time manager, but you may find the remainder of this chapter of interest to you as it will help you to review how you currently plan your time.

**30–37 points**: You are managing your time fairly well, but sometimes feel overwhelmed. We suggest that you read the rest of this chapter, as there will be tips in it you may find helpful.

**25–36 points**: Your degree course is likely to be stressful and less than satisfying unless you take steps to manage you time more effectively. We suggest, therefore, that you read the rest of this chapter and attend any time management workshops organized by your institution.

**0–24 points**: We suggest you read the rest of this chapter and attend any time management workshops organized by your institution. You might also want to talk to a learning support adviser at your institution about developing a personal time management action plan.

## Time management issues

There are **three big time management issues for students**: planning, procrastination and perfectionism (see Figure 8.1). We discuss each issue in turn.

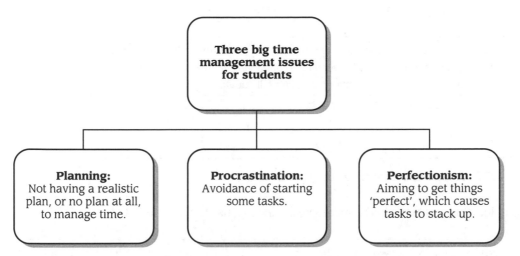

Figure 8.1 **Three time management issues**

### Planning

Most time management problems are caused by students having no clear plans, or having plans that are vague and unrealistic. This can result in students falling behind with reading or writing tasks.

### Exercise 8.1: Planning problems

Planning related difficulties can happen for one or more of the following reasons. Tick either 'Yes' or 'No' for those that apply to you.

| Problem | Yes | No |
| --- | --- | --- |
| 1   I have not had much or any experience of managing time independently in the past. | | |
| 2   I have difficulty in motivating myself to go to the trouble of producing realistic plans. | | |
| 3   I do not have much sense of the time it takes to accomplish tasks. | | |

| | | | |
|---|---|---|---|
| 4 | I come from a family or community that is relaxed about time, which may be in conflict with the time norms of the institution. | | |
| 5 | I am studying in a second language and think this slows my progress on tasks, particularly reading. | | |
| 6 | I have difficulties balancing paid employment with my study responsibilities. | | |
| 7 | Additional responsibilities: I have a family or other carer responsibilities that can create planning dilemmas. I may have planned ahead for the week, but a domestic crisis can overturn the best of intentions and carefully crafted plans. | | |

---

### Exercise 8.2: Resolving two planning problems

Now complete this grid: write in the spaces below in response to the tasks set.

| With regards to planning, the **two things** I would like to change the most are: | My own thoughts, at this stage, on **how** I might begin to change are: |
|---|---|
| 1 | |
| 2 | |

There is more discussion on planning later in the chapter.

### Procrastination

Procrastination is the avoidance of starting a task. For some, it can become a habitual way of responding to some, many, or most tasks.

**Exercise 8.3: Procrastination problems**

Procrastination related difficulties can result from one or more of the following. Tick either 'Yes' or 'No' for those that apply to you.

| Problem | Yes | No |
|---|---|---|
| 1   Other students around me are doing or saying things that appear to be more interesting. | | |
| 2   I struggle to make sense of a subject(s) I find difficult, not engaging, or irrelevant. | | |
| 3   I am anxious about what is expected of me by tutors. | | |
| 4   I worry about failure: | | |
| 5   My response to tasks can be affected by feelings ranging from depression to 'just not being in the mood'. | | |
| 6   I am inclined to rebel against the dictates of others, which makes me reluctant to start tasks not initiated by myself. | | |
| 7   I can feel overwhelmed or 'frozen' by all the tasks I face. | | |
| 8   I can experience boredom, or an aversion to some of the subjects I have to study. | | |
| 9   I am impulsive and easily swayed from one task to another. | | |
| 10   I underestimate the time needed to complete tasks. | | |
| 11   I enjoy working under pressure. | | |
| 12   I do not like to be still or seated for too long. | | |
| 13   I have got into a habit of avoiding unpleasant tasks. | | |
| 14   I don't like having my life dictated by the demands of others. | | |

### *Not all procrastination is a bad thing*

There are some situations when procrastination can be a positive response to situations:

- When the outcome of an action is uncertain and potentially dangerous.
- When unfair demands are being made of my time.
- When a breathing space is needed to avoid flaring up in anger against someone.
- When a hasty reaction might have a prejudicial impact on me or others.

Some students argue, too, that they procrastinate strategically to spur themselves to produce creative work. But you need to be honest – do you **really** produce good work under pressure? Or is this just a rationalization of your behaviour? If you make this claim, can you prove it by comparing work written under pressurized and unpressurized time conditions?

---

#### Exercise 8.4:  *Resolving two procrastination problems*

Now complete this grid: write in the spaces below in response to the tasks set.

| With regards to procrastination, the **two things** I would like to change the most are: | My own thoughts, at this stage, on **how** I might begin to change are: |
|---|---|
| 1 | |
| 2 | |

---

There is more discussion on procrastination later in the chapter.

### Perfectionism

Most people want to do a good job and be rewarded by others for their efforts. This is healthy. But flawed perfectionism is about a compulsive and unremitting drive towards an impossible goal, and about measuring one's own worth exclusively in terms of what you have accomplished.

### Exercise 8.5: *Perfectionism problems*

Perfectionism related difficulties can result from one or more of the following. Tick either 'Yes' or 'No' for those that apply to you.

| Problem | Yes | No |
|---|---|---|
| 1   I want to live up to other people's standards. | | |
| 2   I want to live up to an unflawed image I have of myself. | | |
| 3   I am driven largely by work related goals and find it difficult to relax away from work tasks. | | |
| 4   I have built up a reputation as someone always hard-working and capable; I don't want to do things that risk damaging this self-image. | | |
| 5   I have a real fear of being seen by others to make mistakes. | | |
| 6   I hate criticism and will strive unremittingly to avoid it. | | |

### Exercise 8.6: *Resolving two perfectionism problems*

Now complete this grid: write in the spaces below in response to the tasks set.

| With regards to perfectionism, the **two things** I would like to change the most are: | My own thoughts, at this stage, on **how** I might begin to change are: |
|---|---|
| 1 | |
| 2 | |

There is more discussion on perfectionism later in the chapter.

### Getting control

Gaining a sense of what time you have at your disposal is a starting point for gaining more control of your life. For **procrastinators**, or students with **planning** issues to resolve, a sense of what time they actually have available can motivate them to begin to manage it better. **Perfectionists** may realize too that there has to be a physical limit to the time spent on any one task.

The big issue for students who have difficulty with planning is about how they can best use the time they have within their own control, i.e. free time, for independent study purposes. They know when they have to go to lectures and tutorials – that is not the problem; the issue for them is about making effective use of other time, so that course work and revision is done in good time.

### Exercise 8.7: Where does the time go?

Do you know how much time you have each week for independent work? Try this exercise. There are 168 hours in a week. Start by calculating the estimated time you spend on the following activities.

| Activity | Calculation | Subtotal |
|---|---|---|
| Number of hours sleeping each night. | × 7= | |
| Number of hours per day grooming (washing; grooming; dressing). | × 7= | |
| Number of hours for meals/snacks per day, including preparation time. | × 7= | |
| Total travel time (weekdays). | × 5= | |
| Total travel time (weekends). | × 2= | |
| Number of hours of paid employment per week. | | |
| Estimated number of hours in scheduled lectures and tutorials per week. | | |
| Number of hours on average per week on leisure activity. | | |
| Other things you have to do, e.g. chores, domestic, family responsibilities, voluntary work, etc. | | |

**Subtotals =**

Plus 7 hours extra for leeway:          **+ 7 =**

**Grand total =** ☐

As stated earlier, there are 168 hours in any week. Deduct the total committed hours from 168 to give you an approximate idea how much free time you have left for independent study and course work.

Deduct total hours = ☐ from 168 = ☐ free time.

## The 4-D Approach

If you are a student with significant commitments and responsibilities outside of your course, you may not have been surprised to see how little time you have for independent study. If you are in this situation you may have to adopt a 4-D approach to managing your time:

1  **De-commitment**: identifying things that do not really need doing, and abandoning these.
2  **Deferment**: putting things off until after exams or assignments have been completed.
3  **Downgrading**: doing things to a less perfect standard.
4  **Delegation**: negotiating with others to do things that you previously felt to be your responsibility.

### Exercise 8.8:  Using the 4-D approach in your own life

Think about how you might do that. Write in the spaces below how you might apply the 4-D model to your own life.

| De-commitment | Deferment |
|---|---|
|  |  |

| Downgrading | Delegation |
|---|---|
|  |  |
|  |  |

## Planning: getting started

Some commentators advise that you should keep a record of how you employ your time over a day or a week, so you can see how well (or not) you have used it. Although this is sound advice and can highlight interesting areas for improvement, few people (outside of time management classes) have the patience to do this! The most effective and sustainable time management systems are those that are the simplest and make the task of managing your time as easy as possible.

There are three elements to scheduling and prioritizing time:

- Taking a long-term view.
- Organizing and prioritizing tasks.
- Making a daily schedule of tasks.

### Taking a long-term view

At the start of any semester begin by recording in a diary or time sheet the dates of important events, e.g. exams and assignment submission dates. Blank calendars can be downloaded free from the Internet. You need to review these on a weekly basis, as what seemed like a long time into the future when you recorded it, now may be imminent.

### Organizing and prioritizing tasks

Above all, prioritizing is the key to the effective management of time. It involves reviewing your tasks for a particular short-term period and prioritizing all the tasks you need to accomplish in that time period. These can be grouped into three categories: 'Priority', 'Important' and 'Pending'. You can divide a large sheet of paper into three columns using these categories as headings (see the example that follows).

You can use self-adhesive stickers to list and rank the items in the columns.

You start by reviewing all your tasks in the time period and label one task per sticker. These can then be distributed across the three columns of the poster.

| Priority | Important | Pending |
| --- | --- | --- |
|  |  |  |

The priority column tasks are those that you need to do first and you would rank these, with the most urgent task at the top. The important column contains tasks that need to be completed soon, but the Priority tasks are the ones you will work on first. The Important tasks need some time allocating to them on a regular basis, but the Priority tasks will need a more sustained time commitment from you.

### Making a daily schedule of tasks

You can allocate tasks on a weekly and daily basis using the type of calendar or daily 'to do' list shown.

|       | Sunday | Monday | Tuesday | Wednesday | Thursday | Friday | Saturday |
|-------|--------|--------|---------|-----------|----------|--------|----------|
| 6.00  |        |        |         |           |          |        |          |
| 7.00  |        |        |         |           |          |        |          |
| 8.00  |        |        |         |           |          |        |          |
| 9.00  |        |        |         |           |          |        |          |
| 10.00 |        |        |         |           |          |        |          |
| 11.00 |        |        |         |           |          |        |          |
| 12.00 |        |        |         |           |          |        |          |
| 13.00 |        |        |         |           |          |        |          |
| 14.00 |        |        |         |           |          |        |          |
| 15.00 |        |        |         |           |          |        |          |
| 16.00 |        |        |         |           |          |        |          |
| 17.00 |        |        |         |           |          |        |          |
| 18.00 |        |        |         |           |          |        |          |
| 19.00 |        |        |         |           |          |        |          |
| 20.00 |        |        |         |           |          |        |          |
| 21.00 |        |        |         |           |          |        |          |
| 22.00 |        |        |         |           |          |        |          |
| 23.00 |        |        |         |           |          |        |          |
| 24.00 |        |        |         |           |          |        |          |

### Daily list

Once you have a time plan over a block period, you can then look at a daily plan. A simple daily organizer is all that is needed. You can gain a real sense of satisfaction from crossing out tasks which have been completed.

> *To Do Today*
>
> *Read the chapter on Maslow*
>
> *Practise using EndNote*
>
> *Make a start on the Introduction to assignment 3.*
>
> *Meet Zak in 'Seasons' at 4.00pm*

However, the number of daily tasks scheduled should be **manageable** for any one day, and should be based on a realistic assessment of your time availability, otherwise you will get stressed. Be fair to yourself – don't give yourself more daily tasks than you can realistically manage.

### Procrastination and distraction

As suggested earlier in this chapter, procrastination is about putting off or avoiding a task that you know needs to be done. A study by O'Brien (2002) suggested that over one-third of students feel that procrastination is a significant problem for them. In another study, Taraban et al. (1999) found that many students tended to concentrate their work close to academic deadlines and failed to make use of learning support services and resources earlier in the semester.

Burka and Yuen (1983) suggested that procrastination occurs because it is often a means of distancing oneself from stressful activities; the most difficult tasks are often put to one side mentally until the last possible moment. However, they argued that recognizing, understanding and dealing with why some tasks can seem more stressful than others assists in reducing procrastination.

Allowing yourself to become distracted is a part of the procrastination cause and effect jigsaw. Sometimes you need distractions after a sustained period of study; it is your mind's way of saying 'I've had enough for one day, switch me off!' However, if distractions are deflecting you from **starting** work, or your mind continually wanders from your reading, then you need to think why this is happening.

### Exercise 8.9: Personal examples of procrastination and distraction

If you have a **problem getting started**, what are the things you do, or say to yourself, to put off the dreaded moment? Write in the space that follows.

Once you have started, what things easily distract you from a task? Write in the space below. Perhaps you could think of a recent example and say how you were distracted, and why.

### Getting started

Difficulties in getting started on work are often more connected to your immediate feelings about the task itself, who tells you to do it, and how they tell you, rather than the actual difficulty of the work involved. If you have problems getting started with course work, try one or both of the following strategies to get started.

If you are not attracted to a particular task and are tempted to procrastinate, try this idea: give yourself just **15 minutes** to tackle one relatively easy task. At the end of this time, see how you feel. The chances are you will have gained momentum from the short study period and you will want to continue. Motivation can come **from** action; it does not always have to precede it!

### Avoiding distractions

You could try one or more of these ideas for avoiding distraction:

- **Set yourself a short time limit for reading**: 40–45 minutes tends to be the maximum time most people can read before their concentration slips. At the end of the set time, stop and take a break. The relatively short time you set yourself for reading at any one stretch will help to concentrate your mind on the reading.
- **Combine short bursts of reading with active reading**: making notes of the points in any text will help keep your mind from wandering.
- **Make connections:** distraction problems can occur when the subject studied appears totally removed from reality and practical application. So, to overcome this, as you read keep asking yourself, 'How does this relate to real life?' Try to connect the subject to the world about you and your everyday life.
- **Be selective in your reading**: if you find a particular set book hard to follow, try another that offers you a simpler or clearer explanation of the same subject.
- **Walk away from distractions**: if other students are distracting you, go to a place where others are concentrating and working. When others are working quietly, it's often easier for you to do the same.
- **Reward:** give yourself a reward of some sort for completion of a set task.
- **Do not disturb**: signal to others you do not want to be disturbed – put a sign on your door to that effect.

### The flawed perfectionist

Doing your best is about working as hard and as well as you can in the time available; this is a healthy form of perfectionism. Sometimes your talents and interest in the task will lead to exceptional results; other times the results are less spectacular.

The flawed perfectionist will, however, beat themselves up emotionally for achieving less than perfect results. A less than perfect grade will cause them to fixate on a task and spend more time on it than is reasonable or necessary, while remaining oblivious to their own need to rest and keep their life in perspective. One student comment summarizes this paradox:

> I've written and rewritten this essay, maybe five times, and I still don't feel I can hand it in. The problem is that it has taken over my life. I've cut some lectures, left an important assignment for next week, which I know will cause even more problems, and I am spending all my time just endlessly trying to improve this essay. It's crazy because I know it's probably good enough, but I can't help it . . . I so want it to be absolutely right.
>
> (Dundee Counselling Service 2003)

The irony is, of course, that this fixation on a single assignment leads to time management going completely haywire and the flawed perfectionist is left to cope with a personal time-table now out of control, as other tasks stack up.

The flawed perfectionist believes that only the best grades will give them peace and satisfaction. But it does not happen. Living life this way will deny them peace of mind – because demanding 'perfection' from self or others usually results in long-term failure. What seems a perfect result at first rapidly becomes only 'very good' in their minds as they strive for something better, then better than better, and better still. Nothing is ever good enough.

Being this type of perfectionist may also hinder their future chances of success in their professional lives, because they can become anxious 'jobsworth' types, worried about taking any new or creative actions that might produce an imperfect result, or draw criticism to them. The flawed perfectionist, if they get into a position of authority, can also make unreasonable demands on others, which can lead them into conflict with subordinates.

### Saying 'No'

Tackling flawed perfectionism begins by saying 'No' to making unreasonably high demands of yourself or others; demands that produce only failure and frustration. It also means saying 'Goodbye' to the unreasonable expectations of others. A new, healthier way of thinking requires you to choose goals that are easier to achieve within reasonable time limits, and to stop fixating on your faults and flaws.

### Four more tips for managing time

- A chaotic working area can add to your feelings that your life is out of control. If your working area is in a mess, this will slow your progress. You have to hunt around for what you need, wasting time in the process.
- Concentrate on one thing at a time: forget the other things you have to do and just focus on one task at a time.

- Always finish what you start – this gives you a sense of completion and accomplishment. But don't start more than you can finish in one session.
- When you are quite busy – but not very busy – you can produce effective work. The pressure of being 'busy' concentrates the mind on the task, but without the stress that can come from feeling 'overwhelmed' and working against the clock. The art of good time management is trying to arrive at the 'busy' state of mind.

---

### Exercise 8.10:   *What would you say?*

Here are four time management scenarios. Think about each and what advice you would give the student concerned. Our comments can be found at the end of this exercise.

*Zak*

**Zak** keeps missing deadlines for assignments. He tends to underestimate the length of time it takes to complete the different stages of writing essays and reports. What could Zak do about this? Write your comments in the space below.

*Lieu*

**Lieu** often delays starting an assignment because she worries about her writing ability, which leads to fear of getting started. Consequently, she does not leave enough time to redraft and proof-read work, so her writing is full of unnecessary errors. Lieu is afraid of failing, but her fear is leading to the thing that worries her most. What could Lieu do about this? Write your comments in the space below.

*Bob*

**Bob** has a tendency to build a task up in his mind into something bigger than it really is and beyond what is expected of him by his tutors. He becomes convinced he cannot deliver what he thinks is expected of him by the university in the time available. This reduces his confidence, increases his anxiety and, like Lieu, leads to procrastination in starting assignments. What could Bob do about this? Write your comments in the space below.

*Jayne*

**Jayne** finds it difficult to prioritze her time. She tends to get overwhelmed with all the things she feels is required of her. This includes course work, plus the chores she feels she has to do in her household. What could Jayne do about this?

*Comments on Exercise 8.10: What would you say?*

*Zak*

Zak appears to have a poor sense of the time it takes to complete tasks. He could start to time himself with all the individual stages of writing an assignment, so he has a better sense of how long it takes him overall to complete the task, and which stages are the most time consuming. Once he has done this he is in a better position to plan for future assignments, for example by allocating and sticking to realistic time slots for each stage.

*Lieu*

A written assignment does not have to begin when Lieu makes time to sit down and write it. She could begin to note her ideas as soon as they occur to her. Lieu should not worry about organizing her ideas into a readable form at this stage. The important thing is to gain confidence by just getting ideas down on paper or on screen. The more practice she gets at doing this the better. She could also set herself more than one day for writing her assignment and not attempt to try to start and finish it in one session. She could, for example, write the first draft quickly, roughly, and without worrying about spelling, punctuation or grammar at this stage. Lieu can then put the work to one side and come back to it later to improve it gradually. She could also find a 'study buddy' to work with – someone who will give her constructive feedback, and vice versa. There may also be workshops at her institution that Lieu could attend to help her develop her writing ability. She could also read chapters six and seven of this book for more ideas about writing well and with confidence.

*Bob*

Bob is in danger of falling into the trap of flawed perfectionism (see earlier in this chapter). He needs to aim at doing his best in a conscientious way. If he makes mistakes, so what? He also needs to 'deconstruct' the assignment by re-phrasing the task into simple, manageable terms. With assignment questions, for example, he could try writing a mini-essay (50 words) that summarizes the main point he wants to make, or try explaining to another person his viewpoint on the subject. When you do this you reduce seemingly difficult tasks into something within your grasp. Even complex concepts have a **core or key point**. Get to the core, understand the core, and you start to **control** the written task. Bob could also break the assignment task down into manageable subtasks. Often it is the apparent magnitude of the task, combined with 'perfectionism' tendencies, which lead to procrastination. Dividing tasks up into bite-sized chunks can be the way out of this emotional impasse.

*Jayne*

Jayne needs to start by looking at the issue of the chores she feels she has to do at home. Are other people supporting her enough with her studies? If not, why not? Because of her changed circumstances she needs to negotiate with others about who does what in the house. Jayne could also prioritize her course work. For example, she could make a list of the things she has to do in the short and longer terms. As stated earlier in this chapter, there is something very satisfying about having a list of things to do – and ticking these off when you complete them. You start to feel more in control. However, she needs to avoid starting the day with an unrealistically long list of things to do, as this can lead to frustration if any tasks are outstanding at the end of the day.

## Chapter summary: Key learning points

- Remember that there are lots of practical things you can do to manage your time effectively – try out some of the techniques and keep a note of the specific actions that help or hinder your efforts.
- Acknowledge that time is always going to be scarce, so getting used to working to a structured schedule really helps.
- Remember that no matter how good your time management plan is, it is the simple orientations like staying motivated and avoiding distractions that really make the difference.
- Recognize that building in contingencies to deal with unexpected glitches to your planned schedule is always a good idea too.

### Suggested further reading

Croft, C. (1996) *Time Management*. London: Thompson Business Press.
Forsyth, P. (2003) *Successful Time Management*. London: Kogan Page.
Haynes, M.E. (2000) *Make Every Minute Count*. London: Kogan Page.
Levin, P. (2007) *Skilful Time Management*. Maidenhead: Open University Press.
Neenan, M. and Dryden, W. (2002) *Life Coaching: A Cognitive-Behavioural Approach*. Hove: Brunner-Routledge.

# Learning with Others: Working and learning in groups

**9**

## Chapter Contents

## Chapter Overview

- **Analysing your approach to operating in groups**
- **Exploring behavioural balances and consequences in groups**
- **Understanding project management skills and group work**
- **Developing a group project plan**
- **Learning about group leadership**

## Introduction

Studying and learning at college or university can sometimes feel like an isolated, individual, lonely process. But learning is deeply social. From the very beginning of our lives, we learn better by interacting with other people, at least some of the time. This chapter will focus on some of the important things that are worth considering when you are learning, working or studying in groups. Group work can be really good fun, and very motivating, but it can also pose a few challenges.

As well as helping you to learn new knowledge about your subjects, group projects also provide good opportunities for you to develop a range of other skills: communication, negotiation, listing, persuasion, cooperation, leadership and conflict management can all be put to the test when you're trying to achieve something as a member of a group (Biggs 2003: 187).

Working as part of a group can feel more complicated and difficult than working on your own. But there are also lots of reasons why it is worthwhile and in any case, you will probably find that you will be required to work in teams or groups for at least some portion of your time at college – so it is useful to consider some advice about how best to orientate yourself towards working effectively, productively and happily in groups.

### Benefits of working in groups

There are three main benefits of working in groups:

- Working in groups can **sharpen your critical and creative thinking skills**, can help you to **become a more versatile communicator** and **can enhance your knowledge** in a range of different ways.
- In group work you can **draw on each group member's knowledge and perspectives**, which can frequently provide you with a clearer understanding of what you are studying.
- Groups are great for keeping you **motivated and on target** to complete the task at hand as it is harder to procrastinate when working with others.

### Learning to work together: understanding the phases of group development

One of the most useful things to keep in mind when you have been assigned a group task is that any newly formed-group of individuals takes a while to learn how to work well together. That can be frustrating if you are someone who is very task focused. Have patience, particularly at the beginning. You need to create time and space for you to get to know each other a bit, to learn about the skills and ideas that each person is bringing to the table and to find a way of getting the work done that everyone is prepared to sign up to. All of this takes time. There is a well-known theory of group work developed by Tuckman (1965), who says that it is useful to think about four different stages of group development: forming, storming, norming and performing.

- **Forming**: group members get to know each other, break the ice, become familiar with everyone's different perspectives and ideas.
- **Storming**: group members brainstorm, discuss, share and sometimes clash about what the best way forward is, who should take a leadership role and how particular jobs should be done.
- **Norming**: groups settle into a pattern of activity and develop habits and routines that allow them to become efficient and speedier in the completion of tasks.
- **Performing**: groups sharpen and develop their teamworking skills in the interests of achieving group objectives and delivering their assignment effectively.

Your group project is likely to benefit if you keep in mind that there are phases of group development and that you are not going to be able to pull the whole thing together very well unless you spend time getting to know each other, discussing different perspectives, getting into a rhythm of collaboration and learning how to develop your ideas and your skills in cooperation with one another.

If you pace your group work to reflect its gradual development, then it is likely that you will achieve better results in the end.

### Different people, different roles

There is no point in everyone being good at the same thing. Give yourself the chance to explore what each other's preferences are and what role everyone would prefer to play when you are involved in a group task.

Belbin (1981) studied how management teams interacted and proposed various team role types, listed in Table 9.1.

| Table 9.1  Belbin team role types | | |
|---|---|---|
| **Overall** | **Belbin roles** | **Description** |
| Action focus | Implementer | Implementers are people who may be less likely to come up with ideas by themselves but are very good at finding practical ways of making other people's ideas work |
| | Shaper | Shapers are very energetic, sometimes challenging and bring momentum and action to the group to help get things done and to keep people focused on the task |
| | Completer/finisher | The completer/finisher is reliable and good at looking at detail to make sure everything is complete and comprehensive |
| Thinking focus | Plant | The 'plant' is great at coming up with good ideas or creative solutions to difficult problems – less focused on details and more motivated when thinking about challenges or problems that the group faces |
| | Monitor/evaluator | The monitor/evaluator can see the big picture and is accurate in their ability to see how the group is progressing, what is working and what might need to be changed |
| | Specialist | The specialist brings expertise in a particular area to bear on the work of the group |
| People focus | Coordinator | The coordinator helps to keep the group together and helps each individual to focus on their contribution to the group while also helping to keep activities linked |
| | Team worker | The team worker is caring and considerate and at their best when everyone is working well together. The team worker is good at building morale and making group members feel good about themselves and their contributions |
| | Resource/investigator | The resource investigator is good at spotting opportunities for novelty and innovation. Also great at networking and bringing in new ideas from outside the group |

Belbin's (1981) team role types have been developed as a result of years of studying people's behaviour in teams. Not all teams contain all these personal orientations, but it is suggested that if there is a good balance of different roles in a team, then it increases the chances of the team performing well. To find out more about team roles and to discover what your own team orientation is likely to be, check out the Belbin website at **www.belbin.com/**

### Good questions for groups to ask themselves

It is useful to meet regularly, and at the earliest opportunity to discuss and agree the following kinds of issues:

- How often should we meet?
- Can we agree a meeting schedule?
- How will we stay in touch between meetings (email, text, internet site etc.)?
- What are the things we need to do to be ready to submit our group assignment on time?
- How much work or time is each of us prepared to do to get this done and what other competing activities do we have to grapple with?
- Do we need any help from outside the group?
- Where do we need to go to find help?
- Are there any particular skills/resources/ideas in the group that could really help us in the achievement of our goals?
- Should someone be selected as the leader or coordinator of the group?
- If so, how should that person be chosen?

You can use this list of questions as a guide to getting your group up and running. It is also useful to revisit these questions as you make progress together. See also some more detailed ideas about group presentations in Chapter 10.

## A simple project plan

Teams can benefit from a more structured project plan with clear timelines for different activities and tasks. A simple project plan specifying important activities can help to clarify for everyone what needs to be done, by when, and how the work should be prioritzed and paced. A sample project plan is shown in the illustration.

| Activity | Week 1 | Week 2 | Week 3 | Week 4 | Week 5 | Week 6 | Week 7 |
|---|---|---|---|---|---|---|---|
| Receive group assignment and meet with group members | ← | | | | | | |
| Agree project plan and assign tasks | ▓ | ▓ | ▓ | | | | |
| Complete individual tasks | ▓ | ▓ | ← | ▓ | ▓ | | |
| Bring individual tasks together and collaborate to create group output | | | | ▓ | ▓ | | |
| Review and revise | | | | ← | ▓ | | |
| Finalize and edit/perfect | | | | ▓ | ▓ | | |
| Deliver | | | | | | ▓ | ▓ |

## Leadership and group work

Even for a relatively small group task it usually helps if one person within the group is happy to take on a particular leadership role. For practical reasons, it is useful to know who is going to call meetings, give updates and brief everyone about progress, but also, a good leader can do a lot to create a unity of purpose and to inspire, develop and maintain the momentum of the group in a way that can make a huge difference in the group's ability to work together. Some people naturally tend towards leadership roles. Remember that if you find yourself being the self-appointed or elected group leader, then it is also important to negotiate the responsibilities that other people will deliver. Being a leader is hard work, and one of the important things you will need to do in that role is to make sure that everyone else is pulling their weight too.

---

### Chapter summary: Key learning points

- Recognize that working in groups can be motivating and fun, but it takes **communication, energy and time**.
- Remember that groups usually take a while to learn to work together – **so being aware of the different phases of group development** is useful when you have been given a group assignment, project or task.
- Be aware that different people are good at different things: it pays to recognize and facilitate **different roles** that group members will play.
- Agree **ground rules** at the beginning to save time and get people focused as well as **creating shared values** that will stand to the group throughout its existence.
- Have **structured project plans** as useful tools for keeping people on track.
- Ensure someone is prepared to play **an appropriate leadership role** from the start.

---

### Suggested further reading

Payne, E. and Whittaker, L. (2006) *Developing Essential Study Skills*, 2nd edn. Harlow: FT Prentice Hall.

# Presenting in Front of a Crowd: Learning to present your work in public

**10**

## Chapter Contents

## Chapter Overview

- **Finding out about the aims and purposes of making presentations**
- **Gathering resources for your presentation**
- **Using presentations to build skills and to learn**
- **Developing your repertoire of presentation competencies**
- **Understanding the principles of good presentations and some tips for presenting in groups**

## Introduction

Many people find public speaking utterly terrifying. Students often say that it takes a huge amount of courage just to ask a question or to try to answer one in class. So having to deliver an entire presentation on any topic, having to continue to make sense and to sound knowledgeable and in control even for a relatively short amount of time can sometimes feel like an almost impossible task.

There is something about presenting your voice, your ideas, your knowledge or your perspectives to a public audience that can make you feel vulnerable and exposed. If you feel any nerves at the prospect of delivering a presentation in public as part of your programme of study, then you are in good company. Many of the sharpest, cleverest, funniest people in the world often experience the same kinds of fear.

Even if you do not find the prospect particularly terrifying, it is widely recognized that making presentations to small or large audiences is rarely an unchallenging or unproblematic task.

This chapter will help you to put some of the concerns you may have in their place. It will encourage you to think about the things that you need to do in order to ensure that your presentation is as good as it possibly can be, and that you mobilize all your skills to deliver it with confidence.

## Finding out about the purposes and criteria associated with your assigned presentations

Research has shown that students and their tutors often have different perceptions about the purposes of presentations (e.g. Haber and Lingard 2001) and that if these differences persist, problems with the final grade and the performance itself can emerge. One of the most important things you can do as you prepare to do a presentation is to ensure that you talk to your tutors and lecturers about what they want your presentation to contain and what they want it to achieve. Lecturers can sometimes assign tasks like this without being particularly clear themselves about what it is that they want to see. Or even if they are clear themselves, they might not realize how important it is to explain that to you.

It is very useful to have a series of questions that you can pose, even before you start preparing for any presentation that you are asked to deliver. It will make the subsequent job a lot easier, and it will probably result in a better final outcome for you.

Getting the answers to these questions can help you to avoid wasting time or getting fixated on issues that may not be that important, and can help you focus quickly on the things that you really need to concentrate on. In addition, getting the answers to these questions early on not only helps you to become clearer about the nature of your presentation task, but also helps to clarify its purpose for your lecturers/tutors as well.

*Exercise 10.1: Questions to ask your tutors when they assign a presentation task to you*

 What particular skills do you want us to develop?

 What other things should we learn as part of this task?

 Do you have a marking scheme for presentations? What are the criteria you associate with a good, high-quality presentation?

 Are there any aspects of the topic that you think it's particularly important for us to include in the presentation?

What are the common mistakes that presenters make on this topic and do you have any advice about how we can avoid the same pitfalls?

 Would you be happy to have a look at a more detailed outline when it's ready to let us know if we're on the right track?

 Do you have any additional advice about how we should prepare for and deliver this presentation?

## Gathering resources for your presentation

Making a presentation is a different prospect from writing an essay or preparing a report. You are usually free to draw from a wider range of techniques and sources, and, especially if you are able to access technological aids, you can enliven and animate your presentation with a variety of media and sources. Keep in mind that while you should not bombard your audience with too many bells and whistles, the right sources, used at the right time in the right way, can add power and punch to the ideas and concepts that you are presenting. Our advice is to spend at least some time gathering as many snippets or tools or possible materials as you can and use this as your bank of resources that you can draw from as you plan prepare and finalize your presentation.

### *A note on your personal style and nerves*

The anxiety that is often associated with presenting in public often means that people leave behind their best qualities when they are making a formal presentation. Think about the communication qualities that you bring to situations when you are relaxed, when you are telling a story or when you are in comfortable surroundings. If you bring your own personality, your own ideas, your own sense of engagement and your authenticity to your presentation, the quality of the audience's experience will be naturally better than if you hide behind a lot of notes or deliver something that is flat and detached. It is hard to relax, but the more you try to, the better you will be able to focus on the key messages you want to deliver. Do not worry about the inevitable nervousness that you might feel. Research shows that even if you feel extremely anxious at the beginning, once you get into your stride and stay interested in the material and ideas you are presenting, those initial feelings tend to subside. And besides, very few people in the audience sense your nervousness in the same way you might assume they do.

If you are really overwhelmed then try breathing exercises and visualization. Look at Chapter 11, which has some more in-depth ideas about how best to manage stress when it is getting on top of you.

### Designing and structuring your presentation

Like any piece of work, a presentation needs to be structured. It should have a clear series of ideas and these ideas should be linked and delivered in well planned ways. As with writing (see also Chapter 6), at the beginning of the preparation process, it may not be possible to be totally clear about the ingredients that your presentation should contain. However, you should commit to the development of a clear structure that will help to map out and guide you in your preparations and in your final delivery.

As soon as your preparations are underway, very quickly you should be able to answer the following fundamental questions about the task ahead:

- What is the main purpose of this presentation?
- What questions does it pose and attempt to answer?
- What key concepts are you going to talk about and explain?

There is a more detailed checklist at the end of this chapter, but these first simple questions should help to guide and direct your focus and to build an 'architecture' around what it is that you need to do, and how you need to prepare.

### Some principles of good presentations

This section contains some guidance about the kinds of things you should think about when you are preparing for a presentation:

- Avoid hiding behind too much material: talk directly and simply to your audience.
- Keep your presentation brief and clear, and provide backup for more complex ideas.
- Know what you want the audience to remember: give them something that they can take away that helps to summarize and pinpoint your main ideas and arguments.
- Practise and time your presentation.
- Be creative about visuals and the presentation of ideas.
- Remember to pause and slow down, but do not lose momentum.
- Use interactive techniques.
- Take control of the ending.

### *Avoid hiding behind too much material: talk directly and simply to your audience*

This might seem like an obvious thing to do when presenting, but it is often the case that people do not make connections with their audience and they often make the mistake of spending all the time (or at least too much of it) focused on PowerPoint slides or other visuals. Remember, *you* are the most important visual in your presentation: make sure you stay engaged with and connected to the people you are talking to.

### *Keep your presentation brief and clear, and provide backup for more complex ideas*

Do not assume that the more information you can bombard your audience with, the better your presentation will be. It is easy to destroy a potentially good presentation by packing it with much too much detail and losing a sense of the important central messages you want to convey and conclusions that you want to draw.

### *Know what you want the audience to remember: give them something that they can take away that helps to summarize and pinpoint your main ideas and arguments*

While you need to walk the line between convincing and memorable material, and unnecessary repetition, avoid being timid about reiterating and revisiting the important points several times. For any aspects of your presentation that are involved and complicated, prepare a document, a diagram or explanatory notes that your audience members and tutors can take away once the presentation is over.

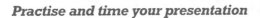

### Practise and time your presentation

It might seem tedious to have to practise, but it really pays to rehearse several times in advance of the day so that you'll know exactly how long it takes. Remember when practising, though, that it is often difficult to replicate the conditions that you will be facing on the day of the presentation.

### Be creative about visuals and the presentation of ideas

Consider using photographs, visuals, diagrams, quotes, video clips and other resources that can animate and enliven your message. But remember, too many of these will dazzle and overload people – so be selective and make sure that you are not integrating material just for the sake of it. Be clear about the purpose and impact of every visual that you use as part of your presentation.

### Remember to pause and slow down, but do not lose momentum

A rushed presentation can really dampen and devalue the potentially great messages and ideas that it contains. Work hard at slowing down; again not trying to pack too much in will really help. Aim for the quality of your message, not the quantity of information. But remember also that slowing down too much can throw you off, disturb your rhythm and can cause your presentation to lose pace and momentum. Try to strike a balance that feels right and that works well for the topics you are tackling.

### Use interactive techniques

Ask people in the audience to share ideas. Make the most of the opportunity to share and develop ideas and stay flexible so that you will be confident enough to improvise in response to issues that they raise. Do not be afraid to admit that you had not thought of a particular angle if someone springs a surprise question on you, but rather use it as an opportunity to stimulate further discussion.

### Take control of the ending

Perhaps because of the relief of having made it through, otherwise excellent presentations often suffer from a lacklustre, hurried ending. You should aim to leave the audience with something memorable, say a powerful visual or a convincing conclusion. Do not let the pace and energy of your presentation drop at the end. Keep your focus clear and wrap it up in a way that your audience will remember and want to reflect on later.

## Common presentation pitfalls and mistakes

As well as the positive strategies we have outlined above, have a look at the most common mistakes that presenters often make:

- Flying through the content at top speed.
- Not having an introduction or a conclusion.
- Not providing time for questions and answers.
- Reading from a prepared text.
- Being overreliant on PowerPoint.
- Being afraid to go into too much detail.
- Worrying too much about ambiguous signals from your audience.

### Flying through the content at top speed

Audiences do not react well to speedy delivery of material. Your presentation will suffer if you try to get through it too fast. You may trip over your words, squash several important ideas into one or two long sentences, get tangled up in some of your most important concepts. It is not always a matter of going slowly all the time. It is usually about knowing when you need to slow down and when you can afford to speed up.

### Not having an introduction or a conclusion

Your eagerness to get into the presentation can be managed by making sure that you tell your audience clearly what your delivery is going to contain and you make sure you summarize well at the end. But you can be creative too. Instead of starting with a series of statements or signposts about what is coming next, you could consider stimulating more interest by posing a question, presenting a puzzle or a conundrum, showing a picture, or telling a story. Any of those devices are more likely to capture the imagination of your audience and help you create an engaged and interested atmosphere which can really set the scene for a strong and effective delivery.

### Not providing time for questions and answers

If you provide time at the end and stimulate a question-and-answer session sometime during the course of your delivery it can really help you to ensure that you cover or clarify areas that you simply did not know required clarification. Always give your audience a chance to have an input. Do not be shy about criticism or questions. The interactive time during a presentation is often the most animated, intellectually stimulating and engaging part of the experience. Try to make sure you avail of the opportunity to get inputs from the people watching you.

### Reading from a prepared text

Apart from very brief, well-chosen text, we advise you to try as hard as you can not to read from a prepared text. The results are inevitably stilted and overly formal. A written text from which you need to read can stand like a barrier between you and your audience. Instead, work to become as comfortable as possible with your material in advance of your performance, so that you do not need to rely on a script. Delivering your presentation using a natural conversational style is by far the best way to make the most of face-to-face presentations, and is much more likely to result in a performance that everyone will evaluate positively.

### Being overreliant on PowerPoint

PowerPoint has become the stock in trade of presentations all over the world. There is now a phenomenon known as 'death by PowerPoint' where audiences are forced to sit through slide after slide of bullet points while the presenter skims through the material relying on the slideshow to prompt their discussion. We are not suggesting that you avoid PowerPoint altogether. Just remember that this too can hinder your ownership of and engagement with the material you are presenting. So if you use PowerPoint, keep the slides to a minimum, and instead maximize your own presence and engagement.

### Being afraid to go into too much detail

Presentations can suffer not only from being overpacked with information, but also by skimming too much over the surface of an issue and not facilitating in-depth coverage or exploration of key ideas, concepts, processes or phenomena. A good presentation can explore something in quite a lot of detail, help audiences to see something from a number of perspectives or encourage people to dig deep in order to critique, question or check assumptions underlying common views on a topic (see also Chapter 4). Do not be afraid to challenge and be controversial. Apply critical thinking to commonly held beliefs about the topic. Stimulate debate and controversy. These are the ingredients of good thinking; avoid being timid about applying them to your presentations too.

### Worrying too much about ambiguous signals from your audience

When you are in the spotlight, it is very easy to get distracted by apparently negative signals you receive from your audience. Frowns, sighs, inattention or other non-verbal cues can really throw you off your game. It is exactly the kind of signal that makes people start 'choking' or 'dying' in a presentation situation. Do not read too much into the body language of your audience. It is well known that such signals are easily misinterpreted and a misinterpreted cue can knock you off balance.

> **Key tip**
>
> **Some advice from the experts:**
>
> We choke under pressure because we are often 'too deliberate' about what we're doing rather than relaxing and relying on our automatic brains to pull out the stops.
>
> Don't try too hard to monitor the quality of your performance while you are performing. It's counterproductive and distracting – just get on with it.

Ratcheting up the pressure during your presentation rehearsals is the best way to get your nerves under control for the real thing. Try to have a rehearsal that, as far as possible, mimics the conditions of the real presentation. Recruit an audience. Have them fire tough questions at you. That way the real presentation will be more of a doddle and you can relax, take it in your stride and give yourself the opportunity to shine.

(Svoboda 2009)

### Other useful resources for presenters

Here are some other useful resources in presentations:

- Stories.
- Pictures.
- Puzzles.
- Examples.
- Role plays.

### *Stories*

Tell a story that illustrates a key theme in your presentation. Keep it brief and interesting and make it clear why it is relevant to the key question or goal of your presentation.

### *Pictures*

Trying to explain something can find you rushing round in circles and overloading your presentation with detail that might be a lot easier to present with a simple picture. Design or select pictures that will shed most light on the things you need your audience to have a grasp of.

### Puzzles

Invoke your audience's natural sense of curiosity by asking: Why is it that . . . ? Or how come . . . ? Or how does it work? Or what is it for? Or what does that mean? By presenting a puzzling question to your audience, you set up the psychological conditions that induce curiosity and motivation – and such conditions provide just the right climate for an energized and interesting performance.

### Examples

If you have abstract ideas or concepts to present, make sure you also offer good examples and illustrations which demonstrate what you mean. So if you speak in theoretical terms ('Supply and demand are important concepts in economics') – follow up by giving a concrete example of what you mean.

### Role plays

Acting out a scenario in order to explain or present important principles of your presentation can be a really great way of engaging your audience. But be careful – a badly rehearsed or half-hearted role play can just cause your audience to cringe. A good one though can be a slick and entertaining demonstration of an issue you want them to understand.

### Group presentations

Presentation assignments are often given to groups of students, rather than to individuals on their own. As discussed in Chapter 9, working in groups can be a blessing (because work is distributed and different people bring different strengths to any group task) but it can also be a curse (it often takes a lot more negotiation, communication, discussion and sometimes conflict, to achieve your task effectively and to perform well).

For group presentations in particular, you will need to do a lot of planning and preparation and you need to pull together as a team and distribute tasks and functions associated with the challenge.

As well as the checklist items outlined in the chapter summary below, which are useful for any presentation task, keep in mind the following additional checklist for group presentations (this would be a useful list to bring with you the first time you meet as a group to prepare your presentation).

*Checklist for group presentations*

1   What are the group presentation requirements? Does everyone in the group have to be part of the presentation on the day, or can some play more 'backstage' roles?
2   What particular skills or opportunities does each group member have? Some might have technological savvy, others might have access to an expert in the area that you are presenting on, others may be good at graphics, others at speaking etc.
3   What is each member interested in doing to prepare for the presentation?
4   How many times will the group be able to meet before the presentation and how much work needs to be done between meetings?
5   When will the group be ready to rehearse the presentation and how many rehearsals should the group plan to do?
6   Who is going to do what research in order to ensure that the presentation is well informed and evidence based?

## Chapter summary: Key learning points

Think about the following questions:

- What materials do you need to gather?
- What research do you need to carry out?
- What are the most important points you want to make?
- What visuals, pictures, ideas, diagrams or examples are you planning to use?
- What critical questions do you want to explore?
- How are you going to engage or motivate your audience?
- How much time do you have?
- Are you going to use PowerPoint slides?
- What are you going to focus on most?
- How much detail will you need to go into?
- Who are you going to ask to help you to rehearse?
- What additional documentation needs to be prepared as part of the presentation?

### Suggested further reading

McCarthy, P. and Hatcher, C. (2002) *Presentation Skills: The Essential Guide for Students*. London: Kogan Page.

# Keeping It Together: Managing stress, staying in control and being ready for exams

# 11

## Chapter Contents

## Chapter Overview

- **Finding out more about what causes stress in your life**
- **Defining stress and understanding how stress affects you**
- **Recognizing the good side of stress**
- **Taking a practical approach to preparing for exams**

### Introduction

Higher and further education is full of challenges and pressures. You may find yourself facing difficulties that perhaps you were not expecting. You will almost definitely need to find ways of dealing with heavy workloads, managing deadlines, and juggling lots of different competing demands. So, like many phases in your life, it is probably unrealistic to expect it to be free of stress.

In this chapter we encourage you to consider some practical and self-aware ways to develop a physically and emotionally healthy approach to learning and study. We explore the nature of the pressures that you are likely to face at least once in a while and we also encourage you to adopt a proactive and stress reducing approach to a well-known source of stress among students – preparing for and doing your exams.

In addition to being a potentially exciting time in your life, college and university life often makes people particularly prone to the experience of stress. Research (e.g. Wintre and Yaffe 2000; Porter and Swing 2006) suggests that stress is increasing among students in higher education. Everyone experiences stress in a different way. What is clear though is that there are simple strategies that anyone can use to make them better equipped to deal with inevitable pressures of life as a student. Your ability to manage stress will form a vital part of a healthy experience at college or university.

## What is stress?

- Stress can be defined as an **emotion**: a feeling of anxiety, tension and worry.
- Stress can be defined as a **physiological reaction**: a 'fight or flight' response capacity to a situation that you find difficult or threatening.
- Stress can be defined as a **cognition** or a **thought** which is based on your evaluation of a situation that you find yourself in.
- Stress can be defined as a perceived imbalance between demand and response capacity, under conditions where failure to meet demand has important consequences.

(McGrath 1970)

So stress is something that has an emotional dimension because it affects how you feel; it is something that has a physical dimension because it affects things that happen in your body; and it is something that has a cognitive dimension because it is both affected by and has an impact on the way you think.

## Understanding stress by exploring your emotions

If you are feeling stressed, it is useful to explore your feelings by asking yourself some simple questions:

- How do I feel?
- What am I feeling?
- Why am I feeling these things?

You might be able to understand and cope with the nature and causes of your stress more effectively, simply by reflecting on your feelings and trying to understand what the nature and causes of those feelings might be.

## Coping with stress through physical exercise

Stress can be self-perpetuating. It is easy to get into a 'cycle of escalation' where you are feeling stressed and then the symptoms of those feelings make you feel more stressed and so your levels rise and it gradually gets harder to keep things in perspective and under control.

A useful way of managing this is to break that cycle by focusing on your physical health. Stress has a direct and immediate effect on your body, increasing your levels of adrenalin, heightening your heart rate, and overall making you quite jumpy. That is because your body is readying itself to deal with a physical threat – even if what you are experiencing may not be physically threatening at all.

Try to make space in your schedule every day for a walk or a run, to get to the gym, or find some other way of giving your energy levels an outlet. Student life can be quite sedentary, so make sure you schedule in time for healthy exercise. People who exercise regularly tend to develop a range of other skills that are useful when you are studying: such skills include confidence, relaxation, stress management and self-care.

## Managing stress by focusing on logic

Just because stress has strong emotional and physical dimensions does not mean that it is irrational. If you feel under pressure, then there is usually a pretty good reason for it. You might be trying to learn material that you cannot understand, you might be worried about money and how you're going to manage financially as a student, you might be trying to keep a lot of things going all at the same time. These are the ingredients that naturally cause stress.

Look at the other common causes listed below and think about which ones are likely to apply to you.

- Leaving home.
- Making new friends.
- Having too much work.
- Struggling with course material.
- Coping with exams and revision.
- Feeling disappointed or disillusioned with your programme of study.
- Feeling overwhelmed by other people's expectations.
- Having to engage in new ways of learning.
- Being afraid of failure.
- Having financial difficulties.
- Suffering from boredom or disengagement.

*Exercise 11.1: Thinking about stressful experiences*

Use the following list of questions to become more consciously aware of the nature of your own stressful experiences.

 What are the things that are causing me to feel stressed?

 Are there any supports at college or elsewhere that might help me to tackle those causes?

 What first steps do I need to take in order to start addressing the issues that are causing me to feel stressed?

 Is there someone I trust that I can talk to who might help me to see things differently?

### Stress is not always bad for you

The occasional bout of stress might sometimes be just what you need at different times in your student life. Although it goes against sage advice to leave things to the last minute, an increasingly pressing deadline can sometimes give you the focus and energy you need to pull an all-nighter and get an important essay or assignment in on time. The occasional bout of stress might actually help you to study harder or to focus on something you've been putting off. But even if that is the case, always keep an eye on how you feel – and be prepared to take action if you start to experience any of the following symptoms of excessive stress:

* Changes in sleep patterns; taking longer to fall asleep, sleeping fitfully, waking up tired.
* Feelings of reduced self-esteem and self-worth.

- Changes in eating patterns.
- Increased difficulty in getting things done.
- Feeling more disorganized and chaotic than is normal for you.
- Feeling persistently under time pressure.
- Difficulty in concentrating.
- Mood swings: often and suddenly feeling angry, tearful or panicky.

Think of how the causes of your stress fit into the bigger picture of your life. Try to put your stressors into a wider context in order to make more sense of them and to gain more control over how you can best respond. Some problems can be put in perspective by asking yourself the following kinds of grounding questions:

- Will things seem so bad in six months' time?
- How big is this problem really?
- How can I break this problem down into different pieces so that I can deal with it more easily?
- What specific actions can I take to try to make things feel more under control?
- What are my most important priorities and how can these help me to look more clearly at the things that are stressing me out?

Even if you are good at putting stressful situations and experiences in context, remember that not all stressful issues are possible to overcome on your own. Always be prepared to look for help when you know you need it.

### Keeping a record to help you reflect on and make sense of stressful experiences and events

Researchers have found that 'writing therapy' is an effective way of dealing with stress, particularly among students (e.g. Pennebaker 1997). Keep a diary to record how you feel about your learning and your workload. Being able to express your feelings in writing provides a release but also helps you to see patterns in your feelings and behaviour. You may discover that your stress occurs at certain points of the week or before certain lectures. Keeping a record can help you to identify times in your week or your semester that you might be particularly prone to stress.

### Keeping a learning journal

A learning journal is a collection of notes, observations, thoughts and other relevant materials built up over a period of time and usually accompanies a period of study, a placement experience or fieldwork.

The notes you keep are a reflection and summary of **what** you learned and **how** you engaged with the process; they will help you can gain insight into the following:

- How to identify or recognize your strengths, so you can capitalize on these.
- How to identify areas for self-improvement and development.
- How to identify ways of learning that suit you best.
- How to gain insight into your potential contributions to future tasks.

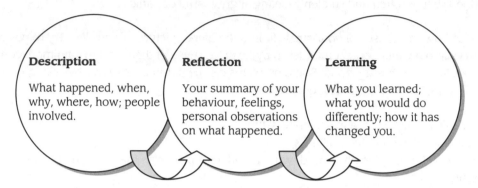

**Description**

What happened, when, why, where, how; people involved.

**Reflection**

Your summary of your behaviour, feelings, personal observations on what happened.

**Learning**

What you learned; what you would do differently; how it has changed you.

Figure 11.1  **Key elements of writing effective learning journals**

The reaction of some students to learning journals is 'Why bother? I can do this in my head. Why should I write it down?' However, the act of writing makes you focus on what happened in a much more systematic, concentrated, powerful and accessible way.

### Avoiding exam fever: planning, preparing for, doing and recovering from exams

Most colleges and universities have widened the range of assessments and assignments that they use to track students' progress. But most still use exams as one of the central ways of assessing learning. So it is worth spending some time thinking about the best ways you can prepare for and tackle the challenges of the end of semester or end of year exam.

#### Long-term approaches to exam planning

Plan for your exams from the very start of your programme of study. Know when your exams are going to take place, how much time will be allocated to each of them and ensure that you are aware of the range of questions, problems, activities that the exam will involve. Ask your tutors/lecturers to provide you with as much information as possible about the purpose and nature of the examinations that they will be setting. The more you know what the aims and purposes of the exam are, the better equipped you will be to gear your study strategies to meet those challenges.

**Exercise 11.2: Focusing on exam preparation**

Use the following series of questions to help you get focused on what you need to do to prepare for your exams.

Questions to help you prepare for your exams from the start of the year

1  How many exams will I have to do this year?

_____

   **a.** Dates                             _____

   **b.** Time allocated to each       _____

   **c.** Subjects/modules          _____

                                      _____

                                      _____

                                      _____

2  Do I have access to past exam papers, questions and answers? What are the most frequently occurring topics and themes?

3  How should I plan my time from week to week to prepare for these exams?

4  What's the best way for me to practise and prepare for the exam?

   **a.** Individual study?

   **b.** Study groups?

   **c.** Practising essay writing under time pressure?

   **d.** Interacting with my tutors and lecturers about exam preparation strategies?

   **e.** Learning to solve problems?

   **f.** Critical reading, thinking and writing? (see also Chapter 4)

5  Can my lecturers/tutors/support providers give me more information, advice or ideas that will help me to prepare for exams?

### Revising and timetabling

Your brain cannot take in, retain and manipulate information in one sitting. Get used to the idea that you will need to revise regularly to reinforce and develop your growing knowledge. Revision needs to be an active process and you should plan revision sessions from the very start of every year. Write up a revision timetable using the time management techniques explored in Chapter 8. Stay on track. Try to balance the time you spend on each module and subject.

Of course also remember that no student has a perfect command over all of their programme of study. If there are areas that you find you have fallen behind on, it is still possible to learn a lot in very compressed periods of time. Some people call it cramming. But if you stay strategic, calm and focused, you can still achieve a lot, even when the exam deadline is looming.

### Generating your exam checklist

- Try to be **well rested** and well nourished before your exams begin.
- Ensure you know the **practical details**: venue, equipment and material you can bring etc.
- Make sure you know as much about the **nature of the exam** well in advance: how many questions, how much time, how long or short your answers should be.
- **Read all instructions carefully**: answer the right number and combination of questions and do not miss out on compulsory questions.
- **Choose the questions wisely**: take the first few minutes to read through the whole paper first and consider what is being asked of each question before choosing which ones you are going to tackle.
- **Plan and do a rough outline for each question**: this allows you to write down all the key concepts that address the question being asked and will help you to impose your own structure on your essays and answers.
- **Budget your time wisely**: allocate time for each question and resist the temptation to spend extra time on answers you think you know well. Remember time spent should roughly reflect the marks assigned to each question/section of the exam.
- **Check through**: try to save some time at the end of the exam to go through the paper and check for any mistakes or omissions.

Face to face with the exam – your summary strategy

Read all the questions

⇓

Be sure about how many questions you are required to answer

⇓

Decide which questions you are going to tackle and in what order

⇓

Plan and outline each answer

⇓

Write each answer

⇓

Move on to the next question

⇓

Review your answers

## Chapter summary: Key learning points

- Be aware that **stress is a normal part of life**, and that **there are positive things you can do to manage it** if it starts getting out of control.
- **Manage your time** by developing a schedule that provides for academic, social and physical time: keep in mind the time management techniques outlined in Chapter 8.
- Eat a **healthy and balanced diet** to keep your brain in top gear.
- Practise **positive thinking** as an important tool in stress management.
- Be willing to **do something proactive to tackle problems** or challenges that you may experience, especially in the lead up to exams.
- Have **someone you trust to talk to**: if you feel very isolated or alone, find out what confidential services there are for you to avail of when the going feels tough.

### Suggested further reading

Lashley, C. and Best, W. (2001) *12 Steps to Study Success*. London: Continuum.

Pennebaker, J.W. (1997) Writing about emotional experiences as a therapeutic process. *Psychological Science* 8(3): 162–166.

Price, G. and Maier, P. (2007) *Effective Study Skills: Unlock your Potential*. Harlow: Pearson Longman.

# 12 Working with Numbers: Mathematics and numerical competence

## Chapter Contents

## Chapter Overview

- **Understanding numbers and numeracy**
- **Adjusting to maths at college and university**
- **Exploring problem solving and abstract thinking**
- **Overcoming anxiety about maths**

## Introduction

Students often find mathematics their most difficult and troublesome subject. It is difficult to avoid maths-related study, no matter what programme of study you have undertaken, and if, like many students, you find that mathematics subjects worry and confuse you, reading this chapter will help you to generate useful strategies for tackling your maths-related learning.

This chapter presents an understanding of the study of mathematics at university the chapter does not focus on those students studying for a maths degree but rather presents tips and tricks for those who are studying maths as part of their degree programme.

## Numbers and numeracy

Numbers present information in a very condense and abstract form. However, we live in a society which communicates information to us in numerical format every day. Sometimes these numbers are presented simply and on their own, for example, when a newsreader tells us the number of casualties after an accident. Sometimes numbers come in sets which are presented together, such as cooking instructions or changes in temperature over the course of a day, or figures on how much money people spend over a particular period of time. And sometimes numbers are put together in the form of a chart or graph, such as in pie charts or bar graphs. Such charts can represent such information as political opinion, numbers of students starting college in different years or rates of pay in different types of profession.

A number on its own does not mean very much. You have to learn how to read it, find out how it can be used and what it represents. 'Numeracy' can be defined as comfort and competence with numbers. Numeracy is a very important competence for you to develop, particularly during your time in higher or further education. It is not a simple or single ability which you either have or do not have. Rather it is a combination of specific skills, experience and knowledge required to read, use, understand and calculate numbers in various areas and for various purposes. You can feel 'numerate' in one field, but at the same time you can feel utterly 'innumerate' in another. We can usually use quite a wide range of numeracy skills in our daily lives, without even noticing it. Ironically, we tend to be much more aware of numbers we do not understand than those we do, so it is easy to end up worrying that we are not mathematically competent, or fearing that we are never going to be able to understand numbers, formulae or calculations in the ways that maths lecturers may seem to expect us to.

## Mathematics at university

Mathematics education at university level is multifaceted and may include mathematics (pure and applied), statistics, operations research and many more topics. Mathematics does not comprise a single discipline in the traditional sense. Mathematics teaching in universities is often designed for two types of audience – the mathematics specialists or majors and users of mathematics. Figure 15.1 outlines the structure of mathematics teaching in universities (O'Donoghue 2004). There are many key factors that affect mathematics teaching in higher education. Among these are changing economic policy, as knowledge-based societies require higher levels of mathematical competence from all. Unfortunately many students are literally afraid of mathematics, often trying to avoid subjects that they think will have a high maths content. There appears generally to be an under-preparedness of students studying maths upon entering universities.

But university or college maths tends to be very different from school maths in delivery and teaching methods:

- A university maths class typically meets less often and covers material at about twice the pace than at school.
- Students are expected to absorb new material much more quickly.

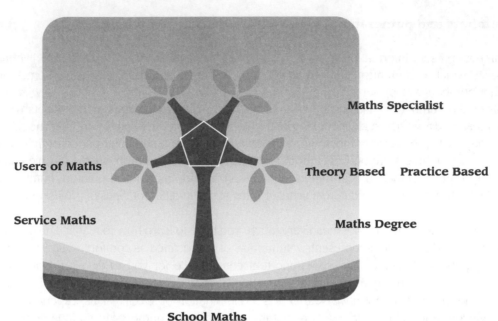

Figure 12.1 **A genealogy tree (O'Donoghue 2004)**

- Exams are probably spaced further apart and so cover more material than before and the lecturer or tutor may not check homework as regularly, as is done in school.

This independent, autonomous type of learning is true of all subjects in higher and further education, but it tends to cause problems in the maths subjects more than in other areas simply because students find maths harder and less accessible. Another complication is that in many ways studying maths tends to be somewhat different from studying other subjects.

### Maths is cumulative

Every mathematics class tends to build on the previous ones, throughout a semester. Students must keep up to speed with the lectures, attend class, read the text and practise new skills daily. Basic concepts and skills are necessary before moving on to more complex mathematical activities. It is very easy to fall behind and to get lost. If you have not got on top of the basic skills and ideas in maths, then you will find it very difficult at the later stages of a programme of study where things get more challenging and more complex. Of course you could probably say the same for other subjects too. But for maths subjects, this cumulative principle is particularly important to keep in mind.

However, if you commit to staying with the programme and keep your confidence and motivation high, you can start to think positively about maths-related subjects. Because each class builds on a previous one, you will always be reviewing previous material and repeating the same formulae and techniques. Identifying and learning the key concepts means that your learning will be principle based, not content based. You will not have to memorize as much.

> **Key tip**
>
> Always remember that mathematics courses are cumulative. Almost everything you do in a maths class will depend on subjects that you have previously learned.

### *Learn by doing*

It is not possible to learn mathematics by just going to class and watching the lecturer work on problems. Like any learning, mathematics is best approached in an active and motivated way. In order to learn mathematics effectively you really have to be actively involved in the learning process; this means doing all the important basic stuff like attending the lectures, paying attention while in class and taking a good set of notes. But crucially it requires that you practise, practise, practise as often as you can. When you learn a new mathematical principle, that piece of learning can be very fragile and easily forgotten if you do not put the principle into practice. So doing mathematical problems (even if the lecturer does not assign any) will probably need to be an essential part of your study strategy for maths and the development of numeracy. When you are assigned maths problems, it is important to practise them, sometimes several times, as they will help you learn the formulas and techniques you do need to know, as well as improve your problem solving skills and habits.

The reality is that most people really need to work hard to pass a maths class, and in general they need to work harder in maths classes than they do with their other classes. If all that you are willing to do is spend a couple of hours studying before each exam then you will find that passing most maths classes will be very difficult.

> **Key tip**
>
> It is important that you are actively involved in the process of learning mathematics, both inside and outside of the classroom. Like everything, but particularly for maths – practising the skill will help you learn to become competent and proficient in this field.

### **Problem solving and abstract thinking**

Problem solving is an integral constituent of mathematics. Problem solving can be viewed as a goal-oriented process requiring the integrated use of a range of higher-order thinking skills, such as generating ideas, making interpretations and judgements, and using strategies to manage the complexity of situations (Kirkwood 2000). Maths continually incorporates and facilitates this type of higher-order thinking (Reed et al. 1988).

---

**Key tip**

When you attempt to tackle a problem, it is essential for you to break down the initial problem and then to develop a sequence of actions to progress and solve it.

---

Problem solving can be approached from two perspectives:

- Problem solving can be defined as the ability to break down a task and reorganize the relationships among object/components to form a solution that works (Yu et al. 2000).
- Problem solving can be viewed as processing previous relevant knowledge learned and applying it to an unfamiliar situation (Cronbach 1988). Therefore problem solving involves transferring and transforming information from previous experiences.

It is generally regarded that through instruction and experience, learners develop problem solving schemas thus enhancing their ability to deconstruct challenges, form mental models of problems and over time increasing their repertoire of problem solving approaches (Polya 1962, 1973).

Problem solving is difficult by its nature. But Problem Based Learning (PBL) experts in all fields (e.g. Barrett 2006) show that learning through problem solving can be one of the most engaging and motivating ways to develop your skills in higher education.

### Breaking down the problem

Mathematical problem solving can be thought of as a bridge, linking mathematics and thinking skills (Stanic and Kilpatrick 1988). Problem solving techniques can be broken into a four-stage process, and you can adopt these stages in breaking down any numerical problem:

- Understanding the problem.
- Devising a plan.
- Carrying out the plan.
- Looking back and reflecting on the problem solving process.

### *Understanding the problem*

As a problem solver, you need to recognize what is being asked, what information is given, what is missing and what are the conditions? At this stage the problem solver should also question the possibility of a solution.

## Devising a plan

A plan means identifying the tools that are required to solve the problem. What calculations, computations and constructions will be necessary? Polya (1973) argues that a good plan of action is a major part of the solution to a problem. If the problem is deemed too difficult at first solving a related problem may give insight, or a smaller subset of the overall problem might get you started.

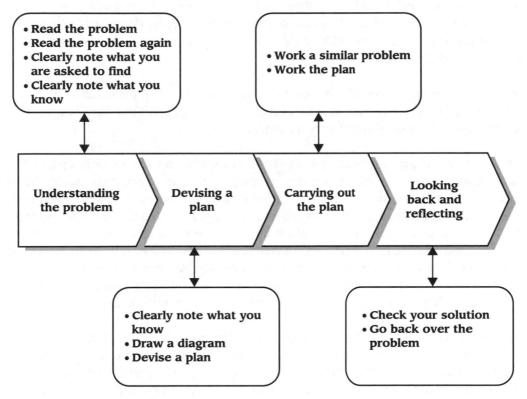

Figure 12.2 **Breaking down the problem**

## Carrying out the plan

This stage is an active process that requires the solver to stick to the plan and to implement it. If a correct plan has been devised in the earlier stage this part of the process is the easiest. If the plan is missing something or has not considered all elements of the problem, then you will need to go back to the second stage and reconsider the elements you have chosen.

## Looking back and reflecting on the problem solving process

This is a reflective stage where the problem solver reflects on the knowledge gained during the problem solving process. Connections to similar problems can be made at this stage.

This phase is useful for developing and confirming your acquisition of new problem solving tools.

### From concrete to abstract

A key component in mathematical problem solving, which challenges some students, is 'abstract conceptualization'. Butterworth's (1992) research suggests that for students to develop abstract conceptualization skills, they need to begin from concrete experience which makes sense to the world they already inhabit (Butterworth 1992). Conceptualization involves interpreting the events which have been noticed and understanding the relationships among them (Petkus 2000).

These ideas are very applicable to aspects of higher education, in particular to numerical skills, where it may be that learning in the abstract and deconstructing problems in an abstract context, can be a cause of much worry and anxiety.

A mathematical object can be concrete or abstract depending on your relationship to it. The meaning we have of the mathematical object is the product of the connections made to other understandings in our mental structure. As the connections between an object and other objects increase, the more concrete our understanding becomes. Therefore objects, which are regarded as 'abstract', can become realistic and concrete if you create numerous ways to represent and link them to your own concrete experiences. Learning to think in abstract ways is not about the dominance of abstract over concrete. Rather it is the interplay between numerical activity and the 'concrete' experiences of the lived-in world. Developing continuity is integral. Mathematical links can be connected with existing understandings.

A feeling of incompetence, a challenge to prior assumptions and a lack of connection to areas in which you feel knowledgeable, may all be sources of anxiety when you are trying to tackle and perform in maths-related subjects. Anxiety can have a huge impact on your learning. The next section expands on the phenomenon of anxiety and links to it the goals of maths learning.

### Phases of anxiety when learning a new skill

**Anxiety is only a phase you're going through. Don't lose sleep over it!** Many students are nervous or anxious when it comes to learning maths and solving mathematical problems. Understanding the cycle of anxiety we progress through in learning a new skill will help to identify methods to overcome any of the maths-related anxiety that you might feel. If you are prepared to work hard and to practise the skills we have discussed above, it is likely that any maths-related anxiety you feel will be short term and with time you will progress to the next stage in the anxiety–performance matrix.

Most students progress through phases of anxiety in learning a new skill, which relates to their effort and performance. Our own research findings imply that students' anxiety changes during the first year of their undergraduate course, as depicted in Figure 12.3.

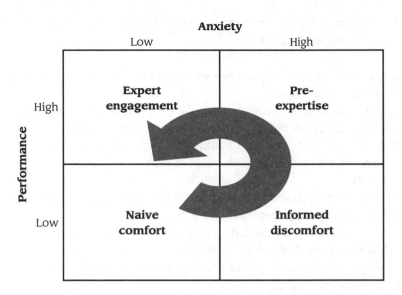

**Figure 12.3 Anxiety–performance matrix for undergraduate students**

Often we have found that first year students in maths-related areas arrive in a state of **naive comfort**, where their performance and anxiety levels are both low. Students at this stage are of the belief that they have appropriate and adequate knowledge, from their limited exposure to the discipline.

As new information is introduced to them, some students progress to the **informed discomfort** phase. Their performance is still low, but as new models and concepts are presented, their anxiety levels rise. It is only when the new information is presented to them that they reach this stage.

The third phase of **pre-expertise** is pre-expert engagement and occurs where students may be starting to engage expertly with the new challenges but still retain residual anxiety as a result of their previous experience as novices.

When the students accept that they need to increase their effort and performance, their cognitive development in the discipline improves, and they enter **expert engagement**. Learning occurs and the anxiety reduces as they accept the new information and become familiar with the new concepts.

## Chapter summary: Key learning points

- **Allocate adequate time for studying and homework:** studying mathematics often takes more time than you may require in other classes.
- **Practise as much as possible:** the only way to really learn how to do mathematical problems is work on lots of them, and the more you work, the better prepared you will be come exam time.
- **Make a set of index cards** with important formulas and concepts to carry around with you to look over when you have got a few spare minutes, and use them to help you memorize the important formulas and concepts.
- **Be patient:** understand that you will not just instantly get every topic that is covered in a maths class.
- Recognize that the only way to really grasp some topics is to think about them and work on them: after a little work a topic that initially baffled you will all of a sudden make sense.
- **Examine your attitude to mathematics:** always do the best that you can.
- Do not do try to do just enough to get by, but tackle your fears and maths-related anxieties and, as always, seek help when you need it.

### Suggested further reading

Bass, A. (2007) *Math Study Skills*. Boston, MA: Addison Wesley.

Northedge, A. (1990) *The Good Study Guide*. Maidenhead: Open University Press.

# Facing the Future and Making Decisions: Planning for and focusing on the rest of your life

# 13

## Chapter Contents

## Chapter Overview

- **Finding out more about your own decision styles and orientations**
- **Reflecting on past decisions and learning from them**
- **Applying different decision making techniques and processes**
- **Using different criteria when making decisions**
- **Planning your future**

## Introduction

The aim of this chapter is to introduce you to some techniques and models for effective decision making and problem solving, with particular emphasis on decisions relating to your career and to your future.

Important decisions can be hard to make. There may be a number of possible and often conflicting options, and decision outcomes, no matter how carefully thought out, can be unpredictable. Decisions are not made in a vacuum; they can affect other people, and other people can have strong opinions on the decisions you have to make.

## What sort of a decision maker are you?

The list that follows identifies eleven common decision making responses (adapted from Rutgers Career Services 2007):

- Impulsive decider.
- Fatalistic decider.
- Delaying decider.
- Compliant decider.
- Agonizing decider.
- Planning decider.
- Intuitive decider.
- Immobilised decider.
- Escapist decider.
- Play-safe decider.
- Deviant decider.

The chances are that you have responded in a number of these ways in the past, depending on the situation you were in and the decision you had to make.

*Exercise 13.1:* **What sort of a decision maker are you?**

Look down the list and think about your responses to situations in the past where you had to make a decision. Don't just think about career decisions: consider all past decisions you have had to make, and tick either 'Yes' or 'No'.

| Decision making responses | Yes | No |
|---|---|---|
| 1   **Impulsive decider**: You took the first most convenient option or alternative that was presented without much, or any, thought of the outcome. | | |
| 2   **Fatalistic decider**: You left the decision open to fate. You are likely to have waited to see what happened, feeling, perhaps, that something would happen to indicate the right direction and that you would be somehow guided to the right path. | | |
| 3   **Delaying decider**: You responded by not worrying too much about the decision and delaying until you really had to decide. | | |
| 4   **Compliant decider**: You were likely to have been influenced by the plans of others and based your own decisions on keeping the peace, or on what you thought was best for the majority. | | |
| 5   **Agonizing decider**: You spent excessive time gathering a lot of information – then got swamped by it. You gathered so much data that you became overwhelmed by the seemingly endless options, which put you back to square one. | | |
| 6   **Planning decider**: You gathered the information needed, analysed it as best you could and then used your instincts to make the final choice. | | |
| 7   **Intuitive decider**: You made decisions based primarily on what you felt; you used your intuition as the main source of your responses to the decisions and problems. | | |
| 8   **Immobilised decider**: You knew you just had to make a decision; indeed, you wanted to make a decision, but you were frozen into immobility because you were worried about the consequences. You knew you had to face up to the responsibility and the decision, but it worried you rigid (and perhaps it still does). | | |
| 9   **Escapist decider**: You tended to escape into fantasy when faced with hard decisions in the past like, 'What career do you want?' You tended to imagine possible futures and decisions that were beyond your short-term (or even long-term) abilities. | | |
| 10   **Play-safe decider**: You made decisions based on the lowest risk, or the safest bet for you at the time. You chose the option that was the one that gave you the least hassle, even when you felt it wasn't quite right for you. | | |
| 11   **Deviant decider**: You were inclined to be a bit of a rebel when it came to decision time. If someone suggested one direction, you were likely to choose the other. You didn't want to appear as if you agreed with others; you wanted to be, or wanted to appear to be, more independent. | | |

**Exercise 13.2:  *Your most likely decision making styles***

Now look again at the styles you ticked as applicable to you. Can you pick out three styles that you feel have recurred in your life? If so, rank them in the grid with the most relevant to you as number 1.

| 1 | |
|---|---|
| 2 | |
| 3 | |

**Exercise 13.3:  *Past decisions you now regret***

Can you think of one or two particular past decisions you now **regret making**? What went wrong? Write in the spaces below.

| Decision made | What went wrong? | Decision making style adopted |
|---|---|---|
| | | |

In retrospect, what would have been a more appropriate decision making style to have adopted for the particular decision(s), and why? Write in the spaces below.

| In retrospect, a more appropriate decision making style for this decision(s) would have been: | This is because: |
| --- | --- |
| | |

### Decision making ingredients

Decision making is an imperfect science and will always be so; the 'unexpected' in life can't be avoided. But as a general rule, the best decisions can often be made based on a blend of the following ingredients:

- **Information**: gathering and analysing the best information from reliable sources.
- **Intuition**: tapping into your instincts about what feels right for you.
- **Self-interest**: doing what you feel will benefit you.
- **Regard for others**: at the same time, having regard for the opinions of others.

## Seven steps in the decision making process

There are seven main steps in the decision making process.

1 Be clear about the decision that needs to be made.
2 Gather the information.
3 Analyse the information gathered.
4 Weigh up the options.
5 Decide which is likely to be the best option.
6 Work out an action plan.
7 Review and monitor your progress.

It looks very logical doesn't it? And it is 'logical', but we cannot always think rationally when we are in difficult or confusing situations, and so steps 4 and 5 are the toughest for most people. However, the following techniques will help you to solve problems and make tough decisions. They can be grouped into two types: structured and unstructured.

## Structured and unstructured decision making techniques

- **Structured**: involving an organized and sequential approach to making decisions.
- **Unstructured**: involving a more fluid approach.

The **structured** techniques described in this chapter are:

- Balance sheet approach.
- Five Thinking Hats.
- Decision trees.
- SWOT analysis.

The **unstructured** techniques described in this chapter are:

- Free-fall thinking.
- Creative visualization.

Three of these techniques – Free-fall thinking, Balance sheet approach and Decision trees – will be illustrated in a case study, Mia's dilemma.

**Case study: Mia's dilemma**

Mia is in her final year at university and has the offer of a permanent job, which pays well – but she is not sure if it is right for her. There is a postgraduate course that appeals to her. Mia is also drawn to living and working in Italy, but doesn't know what type of work she would do there. She likes the country, speaks some Italian, but not fluently, has an Italian boyfriend and could stay with him and his parents. Her parents are not keen on this option; they are encouraging her to take the good job. Mia has been offered a place on the postgraduate course, and she thinks she would enjoy it. It would be expensive, although she could get a loan to pay the fees.

**Free-fall thinking**

The idea and process of free-fall thinking has recurred in this book, because it is an idea that works well in a range of situations. It is an idea-stimulation technique for resolving complex situations, including difficult decisions.

### *How it works*

There are several ways to make this technique work well for you:

- Get rid of normal constraints to thinking: loosen up your thinking.
- Suspend judgement: do not criticize your own ideas.
- Produce as many ideas as possible.
- Use one idea as a take-off point for others.
- Wild ideas are often good ideas: kernels of truth or insights are often found within them.

### *Getting started*

- Take a large sheet of paper and first write down the choices or decisions to be made.
- You could start with one choice option then write down the **first thoughts and feelings that come into your head** in relation to that choice.
- Write down the other choice option(s), and do the same.
- Go back and forth between the options adding to them as additional thoughts occur to you.

The solutions may not emerge, but the issues and problems will often become clearer.

### *Using prompts*

Some prompts to this process could be to think about the following:

- **Risk (financial or emotional)**: what are the risks attached to the choice options?

- **Information**: have I all the information I need? Is the information from reliable sources? Is it up-to-date and free from bias?
- **Values**: are my personal values having an effect on my thinking in some way? Is this good? Or is it distorting my perception in some way?
- **Instinct**: what are my gut feelings about the choices?
- **Other people**: what do they think? Does it matter? If so, why?

### Mia's dilemma: Free-fall thinking

Mia's first strategy is to think freely and creatively about her dilemma.

---

**Choices:** Take job in UK; **or** go to Italy and take any job I can find; **or** take up the offer of the PG course ???

**Italy** – could live with G's parents – could probably get bar work, but my Italian still pretty weak; maybe I could become a tour rep? I need to check this out. What else? TEFL ?? – I need to check this out. Would my weak Italian be a problem?

Italy = ☺☺☺ = favourite option!! SUN/SEA. But work is the issue.

**PG course** – I like the idea of the course = ☺☺ and Parents OK with this, too

. . . but more debt (£4000), and what about job prospects at the end? – I need to check this out.

**Job in UK** – this will please Mum! ☺ . . . Good money = pay off debts/take driving lessons ☺; **But** . . . the boss/other workers look miserable! ☹☹ – is this work **really** for me? Once I am stuck in a job with good money, it's going to be difficult to move out into something else more interesting??

SO . . .

Italy ☺☺☺ PG Course ☺☺☺ UK Job ☺☹☹

---

### Balance sheet approach

The balance sheet approach is a technique taken from the commercial world, where balance sheets are used to weigh up the assets, advantages and disadvantages of any venture.

### How it works

- You list the 'for' and 'against' of the choice options you have identified.
- The technique can be refined by going back over the 'for' and 'against' columns and weighting each item with a score out of 10 according to its importance to you, and add up the total scores for each column (see Mia's example that follows).
- For this to really work, you need to be objective: you need to listen to your heart and your head.

### Mia's dilemma: Balance sheet approach

After free-fall thinking Mia decides to look more closely at her options. Free-fall thinking has been useful for shaking options to the surface. Now she uses the balance sheet approach to look at them in a more systematic way.

*Option 1: Job offer in Britain*

| For | Against |
|---|---|
| The money: **8** | It looks boring: **9** |
| Can afford to go to Italy regularly for holidays: **8** | It's not really what I want: **9** |
| It's a job: **7** | (I don't know what I really want yet) |
| Money will pay for driving lessons: **7** | I didn't like the look of the guy in charge: **7** |
| Pay off loan: **6** | They all looked miserable: **6** |
| It felt good to be offered the job: **6** | I'll be stuck inside: **6** |
| Parents will approve: **5** | I could get stuck in a groove: **6** |
| | I took it because it was offered to me: **6** |
| **Total: 47** | **Total: 49** |

*Option 2: Postgraduate course*

| For | Against |
|---|---|
| I enjoyed the subject on the degree: **8** | The cost: no grant, more debt: **9** |
| I like university life: **7** | It's not taking me in any particular work direction: **8** |
| I can put off the big work decision a bit longer: **7** | Will I like the subject at this level?: **7** |
| Could help generally with career in the future (advanced qualification): **6** | Will I wonder about turning down that job and regret not taking it?: **7** |
| My friend is going to apply: **6** | A cop-out; playing for time?: **6** |
| An easy bus journey to the course: **5** | Time to get a job!: **6** |
| **Total: 39** | **Total: 43** |

*Option 3: Work in Italy*

| For | Against |
| --- | --- |
| I love the country and the people: **9** | The job opportunities for me without additional training |
| I speak some Italian and am willing to learn more: **8** | are limited: **8** |
| I think I would regret it if I didn't go; I need to do this | I liked it as a holiday destination; but would I like it as a |
| while I am still young and free: **8** | place to live and work?: **8** |
| Sun and sea: **7** | I could live with G's parents, but not keen on |
| Culture and lifestyle: **7** | that: **6** |
| I could come back to UK if I didn't like it: **5** | Teaching English, the TEFL course, is an option, but is |
| | expensive – although cheaper than the other postgrad |
| | course: **6** |
| | A leap into the unknown: **5** |
| | I'm still learning the language: **5** |
| **Total: 44** | **Total: 38** |

*Mia's analysis*

Mia's analysis suggests that the UK job is not really what Mia wants, but neither is the postgraduate course, although both have their attractions. The secret of decision making is really to connect with your values and the things below the surface of your life that are important to you – but not to lose sight of the real world; no option is perfect for Mia, not even the Italian one.

If Mia wanted to continue the process of analysing choice options, there are other structured and unstructured techniques that she could try. We now look at some of these other techniques.

## Five Thinking Hats

**Five Thinking Hats** is a structured technique originally suggested by Edward de Bono (2000); you can use it to look at options or choices from different perspectives. This can encourage you to move outside your habitual thinking style and help you to gain a more rounded view of any choice option.

This is important. For example, successful people often look at situations from a very rational and positive viewpoint. This is part of the reason that they are successful. However, they may fail to look at a problem from an emotional, intuitive, creative or negative viewpoint. This can lead them to underestimate resistance to plans, fail to make creative leaps in thinking, and not make contingency plans. Similarly, pessimists may be excessively defensive. And people who rely on their intuition may sometimes leap to decisions without thinking through the full implications.

If you look at choices or a particular problem with the Five Thinking Hats technique, it can help you make more considered decisions.

### How it works

You can use the Five Thinking Hats technique in groups or alone. Each Thinking Hat is a metaphor for a different style of thinking. These are explained below.

#### White Hat

Wearing the White Thinking Hat, you **focus on the data available**. You look at the information you have for choice options and see what you can learn from it. You also look for gaps in your knowledge.

#### Red Hat

Wearing the Red Hat, you **engage your intuition and emotions to** look at decision choices; you also try to think how other people will react emotionally to the decisions you make.

#### Yellow Hat

The Yellow Hat helps you to **think positively**. You take an optimistic viewpoint that helps you to see the **benefits** that flow from the decisions you make. Yellow Hat thinking helps you to keep going when everything looks gloomy and difficult.

#### Black Hat

Use your Black Hat to think about all the **negatives** that might flow from a decision. Look at your options cautiously and defensively. If you force yourself to be aware of possible problems that might flow from a decision, it can help you to overcome them. Black Hat thinking helps to make your plans stronger and more resilient.

#### Green Hat

The Green Hat stands for **creativity**. Your Green Hat gives you freedom to think in a free-wheeling way, without criticism. This can help you to develop creative solutions to any problems relating to a decision.

**Exercise 13.4: *Using the Five Thinking Hats approach***

Try it yourself. Think of a decision you are currently facing, or may have to make in the future, and look at the decision issues while wearing each hat in turn.

| | |
|---|---|
| **White Hat**: focus on the data available; what information is missing? | |
| **Red Hat**: focus on your gut feelings or intuition about the decision; what feels right for you, and why? | |
| **Yellow Hat**: think about all the positives that could flow from the decision. | |
| **Black Hat**: think about the negative things that could flow from the decision. | |

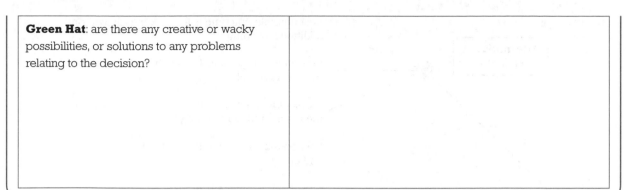

**Green Hat**: are there any creative or wacky possibilities, or solutions to any problems relating to the decision?

## Decision trees

Another technique for looking at choice options is to build a **decision tree**. Decision trees can help you to identify and speculate on a range of possible outcomes, leading to alternative approaches and strategies.

### How it works

You start with one option and build a number of likely outcomes, e.g. 'best', 'most likely' and 'worst', as this can help you to confront issues you may have been avoiding.

Figure 13.1 gives an example of how the 'tree' could look.

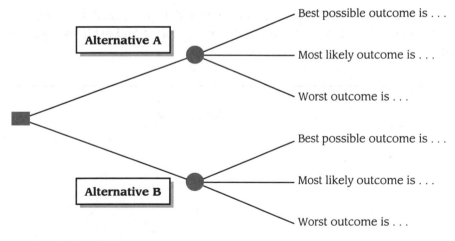

**Figure 13.1  Example of a decision tree**

### Mia's dilemma: Building a decision tree

Mia's 'tree' could look like the decision tree in Figure 13.2.

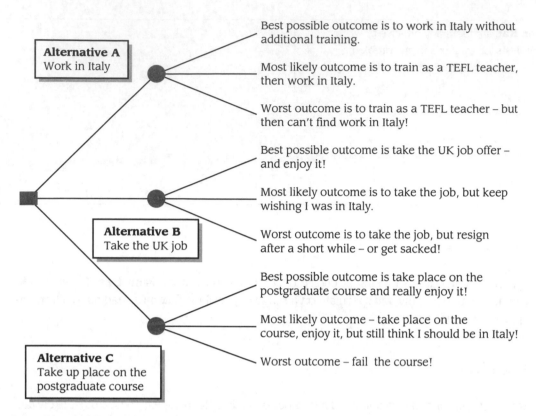

**Figure 13.2  Mia's decision tree**

### SWOT analysis

The SWOT (Strengths, Weaknesses, Opportunities and Threats) analysis is another useful aid to decision making, as you can take each choice option and apply the same series of questions to it.

| Strengths | Weaknesses |
|---|---|
| What are the main attractions and appeals of this option for me? | What are the main disadvantages for me if I pursued this option? |

| Opportunities | Threats |
|---|---|
| In the short or longer terms, what would be the career or life opportunities for me if I pursued this option? | Would pursuing this option create career or life difficulties for me in the short or longer terms? |

## Creative visualization

Creative visualization is a 'journeying' technique advanced by Langridge (2000). He argues that we all have a 'dream', or a nebulous sense of what we want from life; he presents a strategy to help us more clearly envisage what this might look and feel like in the near future.

Langridge's technique focuses on six specific areas of life:

- Home life.
- Career.
- Intellectual pursuits.
- Physical pursuits.
- Family and relationships.
- Our values.

Langridge (2000) feels that a starting point for tapping into goals is to try to separate what is currently **urgent** for us now, and what is **important** for us now, as the important things are still likely to be important in six months' time.

### *How it works*

To help us tap more clearly into our goals he suggests a process of creative visualization. You need to keep an open mind when trying this technique. If you are cynical, don't try it. If you do try it, you might like to combine this approach with a more structured technique, e.g. SWOT analysis.

**Exercise 13.5: *Getting started with creative visualization***

> **Relax.**
> **Put aside any tasks.**
> **Slow your breathing.**
> **When you are ready read on.**

- Imagine yourself five years into the future. What will you look like? Get a mental picture of **how you would like to look**.
- Then imagine walking through a door and discovering yourself in the room where you are living five years from now. Think hard about what this might look like. Where are you? You look out of a window – what do you see? Look for and note details, but don't interpret. Write down your thoughts in the space below.

You look around the room and note furnishings. What do you see?

You walk down the corridor and note photographs of family and friends five years on. Who do you see? Any new pictures?

In the lounge or dining room, on the desk, maybe on a computer, there is something you are working at that absorbs your interest – what is it?

You take a phone call about work. What is the person talking to you about? How are they addressing you – as a manager, equal, subordinate?

A holiday or other event is coming up in the future – what are you planning?

There is a diary by the phone – about something you are going to do that is of particular interest and personal value to you. What is the activity?

You come back to the present – back through the door and review your images. You translate these, if you can, to definable goals. Write these down.

As suggested earlier, you can also use one or more of the structured techniques in this chapter to subject these goals to more detailed scrutiny.

### Action plans

Whatever combination of structured or unstructured approaches you use for decision making, it can help to produce an **action plan**. The process of producing an action plan helps you to clarify goals and work out a strategy and timeframe to work within.

*Exercise 13.6: Making an action plan*

You can use the spaces below to work out a plan to get you where you want to be.

 My goal(s) is/are:

The action steps I need to take are as follows, and should be implemented in the order shown:

| 1 | |
|---|---|
| 2 | |
| 3 | |
| 4 | |
| 5 | |
| 6 | |

### Time schedule

It is useful to work towards your decision goals within a specific time schedule, otherwise things can drift and not get done. At the end of each time schedule stage you can look back to review progress, then look forward to see what remains to be done to reach your goal.

---

*Exercise 13.7:  Creating a time schedule*

Complete the following sentences:

My plan is to reach my goals by

So tomorrow I will:

Over the next week I will:

Over the next month I will:

---

**Over the next three months I will:**

**Over the next six months I will:**

**And beyond that I will:**

## Chapter summary: Key learning points

- Be aware that decision styles do have an impact on the way you approach decisions and on the kinds of decisions you make.
- Think about your longer-term goals, when planning for your future and then figure out what you need to do in the shorter term to give you the best possible chance of achieving those goals – but also be ready to change your plans in response to the unexpected.
- Appreciate that it is difficult to be decisive when your future is uncertain, and even when you have good information in front of you, it is not always possible to make the perfect decision.
- Remember that there are many structured approaches to decision making that can help you to make more sense of the choices in front of you: when you have a difficult decision in front of you, try using some of the techniques we have suggested.

### Suggested further reading

Adair, J. (2007) *Decision Making and Problem Solving Strategies*, 2nd edn. London: Kogan Page.

## Conclusion

This handbook has been designed to provide you with a series of signposts, activities and reflections that we hope will help you to make the most of your time at University. That time is valuable and we hope you have seen that there are ways to use it that really do make a difference to your learning and your success as a university student.

The most vital message that runs through this book is the importance of engagement. Like life, university experience tends to improve the more you put into it. So engage in your studies enthusiastically, be curious, bring energy and excitement to your learning and help others to do the same. And by combining that with the insights and ideas that are presented in this handbook, you can make the very most of the lessons you learn about your subjects, and even more crucially, about yourself.

# References

Barrett, T. (2006) *Learning in PBL as Hard Fun*. Manchester: Centre for Excellence in Enquiry Based Learning, University of Manchester.

Baty, C. (2004) *No Plot? No Problem*. San Francisco, CA: Chronicle.

Belbin, R.M. (1981) *Management Teams: Why They Succeed and Fail*. Oxford: Butterworth-Heinemann.

Biggs, J. (2003) *Teaching for Quality Learning at University: What the Student Does*, 2nd edn. Buckingham: Open University Press.

Blaxter, L., Hughes, C. and Tight, M. (2006) *How to Research*, 3rd edn. Maidenhead: Open University Press.

Borg, E. (2008) The characteristics of academic writing, in S. Moore (ed.) *Supporting Academic Writing among Academics and Students*. London: SEDA (Staff and Educational Development Association).

Browne, M.N. and Keeley, S.M. (2007) *Asking the Right Questions: A Guide to Critical Thinking*. Upper Saddle River, NJ: Pearson Prentice Hall.

Burka, J.B. and Yuen, L.M. (1983) *Procrastination: Why You Do It and What To Do about It*. Reading, MA: Addison-Wesley.

Butterworth, G. (1992) *Context and Cognition*. London: Harvester.

Carroll, J. (1963) A model of school learning. *The Teachers College Record* 64: 722–733.

Clegg, B. (2000) *Instant Stress Management*. London: Kogan Page.

Collis, J. and Hussey, R. (2003) *Business Research: A Practical Guide for Undergraduate and Postgraduate Students*, 2nd edn. Basingstoke: Palgrave Macmillan.

Cronbach, L.J. (1988) Five perspectives on validity argument, in H. Wainer and H.I. Braun (eds) *Test Validity*. Hillsdale, NJ: Erlbaum.

Csikszentmihalyi, M. (1990) *'Flow': The Psychology of Optimal Experience*. New York: Harper & Row.

De Bono, E. (2000) *Six Thinking Hats*. London: Penguin.

Dickinson, D. (1997) *Learning Through the Arts*. New Horizons for Learning. Available at http://newhorizons.org/strategies/arts/dickinson_lrnarts.htm (accessed 5 November 2009).

Dreyfus, H.L. and Dreyfus, S.E. (1986) *Mind Over Machine: The Power of Intuition and Expertise in the Era of the Computer*. New York: The Free Press.

Dundee Counselling Service (2003) *Perfectionism*. Available at www.dundee.ac.uk/studentservices/counselling/leaflets/perfect.htm (accessed 10 November 2009).

Elbow, P. and Belanoff, P. (2000) *A Community of Writers*. San Francisco, CA: Jossey Bass.

Ericsson, K.A. (2004) Deliberate practice and the acquisition and maintenance of expert performance in medicine and related domains. *Academic Medicine* 79(10): 570–581.

Franklin, M.S., Moore, K.S., Yip, C-Y., Jonides, J., Rattray, K. and Moher, J. (2008) The effects of musical training on verbal memory. *Psychology of Music* 36(3): 353–365.

Gardner, H. (1999) *Intelligence Reframed: Multiple Intelligences for the 21st Century*. New York: Basic Books.

Gardner, H. (2006) *Multiple Intelligences: New Horizons in Theory and Practice*. New York: Basic Books.

Haber, R.J. and Lingard, L.A. (2001) Learning oral presentation skills: A rhetorical analysis with pedagogical and professional implications. *Journal of General Internal Medicine* 16(5): 308–314.

Henry, G.T. (1990) *Practical Sampling*. Newbury Park, CA: Sage.

Hjortshoj, K. (2001) *Understanding Writing Blocks*. Oxford: Oxford University Press.

Kirkwood, M. (2000) Infusing higher-order thinking and learning to learn into content instruction: A case study of secondary computing studies in Scotland. *Journal of Curriculum Studies* 32(4): 509–535.

Klein, S. (1971) Student influence on teacher behavior. *American Education Research Journal* 8(3): 403–421.

Langridge, K. (2000) *Mentoring the Dream* (video). Available at www.greenwood-partnership.com/videos.html (accessed 10 November 2009).

Lau, J. and Chan, J. (2006) *Critical Thinking Web: Fishbone Diagrams*. Available at http://philosophy.hku.hk/think/sci/ce-diagram.php (accessed 5 November 2009).

McGrath, J.E. (1970) A conceptual formulation for research on stress, in J.E. McGrath (ed.) *Social and Psychological Factors in Stress*. New York: Holt, Rinehart & Winston.

Moore, S. (ed.) (2008) *Supporting Academic Writing Among Students and Academics*, SEDA special no. 24. London: SEDA (Staff and Educational Development Association).

Moore, S. and Murphy, M. (2005) *How To Be a Student: 100 Great Ideas and Practical Habits for Students Everywhere*. Maidenhead: Open University Press.

Murray, R. (2006) *How to Write a Thesis*, 2nd edn. Maidenhead: Open University Press.

Murray, R. and Moore, S. (2006) *The Handbook of Academic Writing: A Fresh Approach*. Maidenhead: Open University Press.

Neville, C. (2007) *The Complete Guide to Referencing and Avoiding Plagiarism*. Maidenhead: Open University Press.

Novak, J.D. and Cañas, A.J. (2006) *The Theory Underlying Concept Maps and How to Construct Them*. Technical Report IHMC CMAP Tools 2006-01. Available at http://cmap.ihmc.us/Publications/ResearchPapers/TheoryCmaps/TheoryUnderlyingConceptMaps.htm (accessed 5 November 2009).

O'Brien, W.K. (2002) Applying the transtheoretical model to academic procrastination. *Dissertation Abstracts International. Section B: The Sciences and Engineering* 62(11-B): 5359.

O'Donoghue, J. (2004) An Irish perspective on the mathematics problem. Plenary speech, Irish Symposium for Undergraduate Mathematics Education (ISUME 2), Dublin.

O'Neill, G. (2005) Presentation to Seminar. University College Dublin, April.

Parkinson, J. (2007) *I Before E (Except After C): Old-School Ways to Remember Stuff*. London: Michael O'Mara.

Paul, R. (1990) *Critical Thinking*. Rohnert Park, CA: Center for Critical Thinking and Moral Critique, Sonoma State University.

Pennebaker, J.W. (1997) Writing about emotional experiences as a therapeutic process. *Psychological Science* 8(3): 162–166.

Petkus, E. (2000) A theoretical and practical framework for service-learning in marketing: Kolb's experiential learning cycle. *Journal of Marketing Education* 22: 64–70.

Polya, G. (1962) *Mathematical Discovery*. Princeton, NJ: Princeton University Press.

Polya, G. (1973) *How to Solve It*. Princeton, NJ: Princeton University Press.

Porter, S. and Swing, R. (2006) Understanding how first-year seminars affect persistence. *Research in Higher Education* 47(1): 89–109.

Reed, W.M., Palumbo, D.B. and Stolar, A.L. (1988) The comparative effects of BASIC and LOGO instruction on problem solving skills. *Computers in the Schools* 4: 105–118.

Rose, C. and Nicholl, M.J. (1997) *Accelerated Learning for the 21st Century*. New York: Dell.

Rosenthal, R. (1966) *Experimenter Effects in Behavioral Research*. New York: Appleton-Century-Crofts.

Rutgers Career Services (2007) *Make a Decision*. New Brunswick, NJ: Rutgers University. Available at http://careerservices.rutgers.edu/OCAmakedecision.shtml (accessed 10 November 2009).

Saunders, M., Lewis, P. and Thornhill, A. (2009) *Research Methods for Business Students*, 5th edn. Harlow: Prentice Hall.

Shermer, M. (1997) *Why People Believe Weird Things: Pseudoscience, Superstitions and Other Confusions of our Time*. New York: Macmillan.

Simon, A.A. and Chase, W.G. (1973) Skill in chess. *American Scientist* 61: 394–403.

Stanic, G.M.A. and Kilpatrick, J. (1988) Historical perspectives on problem solving in the mathematics curriculum, in R.I. Charles and E.A. Silver (eds) *The Teaching and Assessing of Mathematical Problem Solving*. Reston, VA: National Council of Teachers of Mathematics.

Svoboda, E. (2009) Avoiding the big choke. *Scientific American Mind* 20: 36–41.

Taraban, R., Maki, W.S. and Rynearson, K. (1999) Measuring study time distributions: Implications for designing computer-based courses. *Behavior Research Methods, Instruments and Computers* 31(2): 263–269.

Tuckman, B. (1965) Developmental sequence in small groups. *Psychological Bulletin* 63(2): 384–399.

Wintre, M.G. and Yaffe, M. (2000) First-year students' adjustment to university life as a function of relationships with parents. *Journal of Adolescent Research* 15(1): 9–37.

Yu, C.H., DiGangi, S.A., Jannasch-Pennell, A., Cohn, S. and Collins, C. (2000) Gathering and scattering: A study of the relationship between mental modelling, physical modelling and problem solving. Paper presented at the Annual Meeting of the American Educational Research Association, New Orleans, LA, April.

# Index